A Child
Sees God

of related interest

BIBLE STORIES IN COCKNEY RHYMING SLANG
Keith Park
ISBN 978 1 84310 933 4

THE SPIRITUAL DIMENSION OF CHILDHOOD
Kate Adams, Brendan Hyde and Richard Woolley
ISBN 978 1 84310 602 9

CHILDREN AND SPIRITUALITY
Searching for Meaning and Connectedness
Brendan Hyde
ISBN 978 1 84310 589 3

THE SPIRIT OF THE CHILD
Revised Edition
David Hay with Rebecca Nye
ISBN 978 1 84310 371 4

A Child Sees God

CHILDREN TALK ABOUT BIBLE STORIES

REV DR HOWARD WORSLEY

FOREWORD BY PROFESSOR JOHN M. HULL

JESSICA KINGSLEY PUBLISHERS
LONDON AND PHILADELPHIA

First published in 2009
by Jessica Kingsley Publishers
116 Pentonville Road
London N1 9JB, UK
and
400 Market Street, Suite 400
Philadelphia, PA 19106, USA

www.jkp.com

Copyright © Howard Worsley 2009
Foreword copyright © John M. Hull 2009

Library of Congress Cataloging in Publication Data
Worsley, Howard.
    A child sees God : children talk about Bible stories / Howard Worsley ; foreword by John Hull.
        p. cm.
    Includes bibliographical references (p.   ).
    ISBN 978-1-84310-972-3 (pb : alk. paper) 1. Bible--Children's use. 2. Bible stories. 3. Bible--Criticism, interpretation, etc. I. Title.
    BS618.W67 2009

    220.6083--dc22

                                                        2008048907s

British Library Cataloguing in Publication Data
A CIP catalogue record for this book is available from the British Library

ISBN 978 1 84310 972 3

Printed and bound in Great Britain by
Athenaeum Press, Gateshead, Tyne and Wear

Contents

Foreword

Does the Bible still have something sacred about it in a society where the vast majority of people no longer attend church? If the traffic isn't too bad, the taxi ride from the theological college where I work to where I live is only about ten minutes. A couple of weeks ago the driver, who had not driven me before, asked me about my work. When I told him that I teach people who are preparing for Christian ministry, he told me how his life had been changed by reading the Bible. He had not been brought up as a church-goer, but had been curious for a long time to know what the Bible was all about. He decided to take a copy of the Bible with him in his taxi, and in the quiet intervals between calls, he read it. To my surprise, he explained that he had literally begun at the first page and read steadily until the end. Although slightly put off by the chapters describing who beget whom, he took it all in good spirit and it made a deep impression upon him. In fact, it stirred his imagination so deeply that he began to pray. Today he is an active member of a church, and believes that he met the God of the Bible who has transformed his life.

Such things do seem to happen today but they cannot be very common. The barriers between modern people and these ancient writings do seem to be considerable. Not only is the Bible a big book, but its strange appearance, with numbered verses, pages printed in columns, and the unintelligible contents pages would put most people off immediately. The Bible speaks about a world in which God walks and talks with human beings in a way which seems unrealistic, even magical. Amazing things happen and it is difficult to know to what extent you are suppose to take all this at face value. For some people, the Bible still conveys an aura of holiness which makes it impossible to approach it with an ordinary sense of interest and enjoyment, while for others the stories of violence and killings would be horrifying if they were credible.

In spite of all of this, many of the stories in the Bible somehow seem to retain their fascination. The people of the Bible, whether we think of Adam and Eve, Abraham and Joseph, Moses and Joshua, David and Solomon, Jesus and Paul, continue to shape the imagination, and seem to be saying something to us about how life should be lived. But how can this quality of the Bible be captured today? Is it possible for these stories still to speak to us?

The present book springs from the belief that it is adults who may find the Bible difficult, although my taxi driver friend was certainly an exception. Perhaps it is because in our adult lives we are too busy, perhaps put off by early experiences of church, perhaps discouraged by the image of the supernatural which may still shroud the Bible, that we adults are seldom open to its message. Is it possible that children, who do not have these impressions, memories and presuppositions, might be able to respond to the Bible in a way that we cannot? Can we rediscover the message of the Bible through the ministry of children?

In order to test these questions, advertisements were placed in the church press inviting parents who read the Bible with their children, or would like to do so, to contact us. Of these who responded, about thirty families were selected to take part in the inquiry. Different types of Bible story were selected, and parents or grandparents were given careful instructions as to how to tell the stories and to record the responses of their child or children. As the material began to come in, it became clear that we were beginning to expose a remarkable stream of criticism, creativity and humour. The best of this material is presented in what follows.

Not only does this book illustrate the freshness with which children can still respond to the Bible and the ways in which it can be surprisingly relevant to life today, but it is also a kind of training manual. The parents who read or told the selected stories to their children were not experts in biblical interpretation; they often found themselves in deep water, and had to confess that they could not reply to the questions of their children. Somehow, however, none of that mattered. The three way relationship which was set up between the child, the text and the adult somehow generated its own spontaneity and authenticity. It did not matter whether one was teaching the children "the right" things, or whether what was emerging was consistent with religious teaching. The immediacy of the texts became its own argument, and the response of the children a sufficient expression of faith. It is hoped that many adult readers will be encouraged by these models to try out the same thing with their children.

The work presented here represents another stage in Howard Worsley's longstanding interest in the relation between children and adults. Many years ago I had the pleasure of supervising his PhD research in the University of Birmingham, when he studied the degree to which the faith of childhood could provide a resource for the continued faith of those children in their adult lives. He followed this up with several studies of children's attitudes to Christian faith but his main interest has been in the child as theologian. In the material which he presents here, Howard does succeed in showing how the child can indeed become a theological teacher. The children will greet the reader in the pages that follow, and will present fresh insights to those who read with an open mind toward these classical texts of human spirituality and divine revelation.

John M. Hull
The Queen's Foundation for Ecumenical Theological Education
Birmingham, July 2008

Introduction

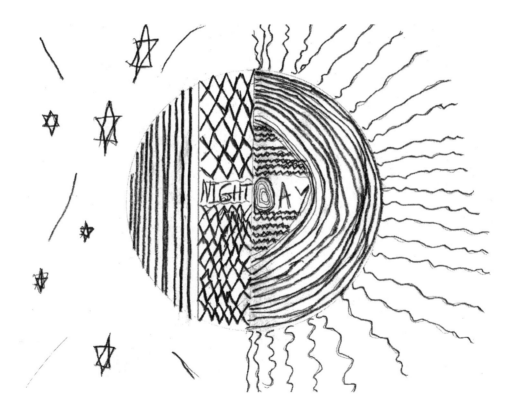

The insights of children

I have always wondered exactly what Jesus meant when he said to his adult followers, "Unless you become like a child, you cannot enter the Kingdom of heaven."

Whole volumes have been written attempting to answer this question; some focus on Christ's concept of childhood, others on the insights of actual children. Still others have looked more metaphorically at how adults can learn from children or alternatively can learn from their own recalled insights that come from remembered childhood.

This book offers a different answer to the question – one found in the voice of actual children as they respond to and engage with particular stories found in the Bible, as read to them by their parents.

The aim is to see if the child's eye view of the Bible could offer a new way of understanding it. The child's interpretation of scripture seen at different developmental stages, provides a different lens through which to view the texts, even if they are complex. On a personal note, there have certainly been times when I have been totally baffled by a story in the Bible, despite having read the commentary, and have mentioned this to one of my children or to a young person and received huge help in my understanding.

The child's understanding offers insights that are hidden from adults, and perspectives that are not obvious to the wise. It is of benefit to those who wish to communicate with young people or to understand them, as well as to those who wish to better understand the Bible. This includes parents, teachers and ministers, or indeed anyone who is intrigued either by the hidden world of children or the hidden world of the Bible.

To understand the ancient text from a child's point of view can be thought of as either an emancipatory act (that releases a text from the shackles of a prior domination) or an exploratory one (that offers a creative understanding from an original vision).

An emancipatory reading of the Bible might be like the Marxist, feminist or black hermeneutics (the technical term referring to the interpretation of religious texts), all of which have their own strong sources of documentation. However, until now the child's insight has not been released as separate from the adult interpretation. The exploratory reading of sacred texts, similarly, is one that is less well-documented and until now has not been taken seriously as being a method employed with children.

This book is fuelled by the sense that children have a unique insight that has hitherto not been focused upon in reading Bible stories. Therefore, what has been recorded is the result of careful listening to actual conversations of real children in the home talking to their parents, grandparents or trusted friends after they have heard a Bible story.

A second aim of the book, after releasing this voice of the child, is to encourage the adult to respond to the child's insights. This response is a return to a former and primal knowledge that might have been forgotten but which is likely to be of resource to the adult.

The story has been told of a small child who asked her mother if she could be left alone in the room with her new baby. The mother was concerned as to what this might be about and refused. However, as the child continued to plead for this privilege, the mother relented and left the room but observed the proceedings through a crack in the door.

The little girl was seen to crawl up to her baby sibling and to whisper in her ear, "Tell me what God is like, because I have almost forgotten."

This book is driven by a similar urgency – to capture what is orignally natural and apparent but what becomes foreign.

Back in the 18th century this same concern was well articulated by Wordsworth in his *Ode on Intimations of Immortality from Recollections of Early Childhood*:

But trailing clouds of glory do we come
From God who is our home:
Heaven lies about us in our infancy!
Shades of the prison-house begin to close
Upon the growing Boy,
But he beholds the light, and whence it flows,
He sees it in his joy;
The Youth, who daily farther from the east
Must travel, still is Nature's priest,
And by the vision splendid
Is on his way attended;
At length the Man perceives it die away,
And fade into the light of common day.

Having identified the need to unlock the child's vision, attention must be given to why its insights been lost for so long.

Why these insights have been ignored

There are multiple reasons as to why adults do not pay specific attention to a child's insights. One of these is that when adults have left the early lands of childhood's Eden, fantasy and play they want to set up a boundary wall around what they deem to be an imaginary world. There is a sense that early reflections emerge from a garden out of which the adult has grown, and to return to it is to reverse the noble pursuit of development. Maybe those who draw on childhood insights are people who have unresolved pathological issues, maybe they have never grown up properly or maybe they are simply sentimental.

Amongst other factors, these reasons have conspired to drive spiritual insights into another compartment of the brain that has hitherto been less trusted. In this way a parent may delight in their child's perceptions but store them deep in their heart rather than discuss them in a more

public forum. Similarly a teacher might be fascinated by the poetic reso-
nances of a pupil but not dwell on these insights too long as the curriculum pathway is followed. Again, within a religious tradition, the priest
or minister might be delighted by the early receptivity of children but
wish to overlay it with a stronger credal code rather than allow it room
for exploration. All of these are ways in which a child's spirituality has
not been empowered.

A closer look at the educational influences on church leaders and RE
teachers offers further insight.

In the 1960s influential research was carried out in schools by Ronald
Goldman (1964, 1965) who concluded that many Bible texts should not
be used with children under the age of 12 because their cognitive reasoning was inadequate. In his words, the texts required a greater readiness
for learning, intellectualism, emotionalism and physicalism.

He went on to describe the way in which the Bible was to be used
was by "a severe pruning of Bible content in the early years" so that children hear stories that relate to their experience and do not get confused
by their literalism.

Goldman was greatly influenced by the Swiss educationalist Jean
Piaget (1886–1980) who was originally trained as a biologist, and
became intrigued by the way young humans construct their understanding of the world. Piaget's writings are based on his detailed observations
of his own three children as they encounter reality and develop through
various key stages of comprehension.

A readable yet detailed discussion of the Piagetian legacy is offered
by Margaret Donaldson's *Children's Minds* (1978). Her summary of the
key criticisms of Piaget's insights are that he gave insufficient emphasis
to the developmental role of language, and that he failed to give enough
attention to the context in which a child was growing. In short, Piaget
failed to recognize the significance of the cultural context on the growing

child as he believed the development of the mind to be independent of the early environment.

These assumptions flowed into Goldman's research on children encountering the Bible. They need to be considered as they have left an enduring mark on how the Bible has been used with children. This book endeavours to demonstrate that the Bible is in fact far more valuable as a text to be used with children than ever Goldman suggested.

Since the 1960s it has been acknowledged that the Bible has been increasingly neglected in most schools in the United Kingdom. Research by Lesley Francis entitled *Who Reads the Bible? A Study Among 13–15 Year Olds* (2000), has detailed this level of adolescent lack of interest.

This ambivalence was also noted by the Biblos Project that researched the uses of the Bible in British schools from 1998 to 2004.

This project was not surprised that young people in Britain were ambivalent towards the Bible, and challenged teachers of RE and the faith communities to work towards giving a more positive view of the Bible.

How these insights can be revealed

The apostle Paul recorded that spiritual wisdom was not apparent to his culture and even appeared foolish. He wrote:

> We speak of God's secret wisdom, a wisdom that has been hidden and that God destined for our glory before time began. None of the rulers of this age understood it … it appears foolish to them. (1 Corinthians 2 v 7, 8 & 14)

Spiritual wisdom is of this quality – not immediately obvious to everyone who encounters it but deeply compelling to those who are struck by it. It seems to me that children are far more open to these divine insights than are many adults.

Elsewhere I have worked towards identifying a child's hermeneutic of scripture seen when a child encounters the Bible (Worsley 2006). In that research I noted that children were more open to receiving new insights from the Bible than adults, because adults tended to be governed by pre-set theological beliefs, whereas children were more wondrous.

This book can therefore be seen as a natural progression of a line of research that wishes to hear the actual voice of the child speaking for him or herself as scripture is encountered.

So how can the child's voice be heard? If we listened only to the voices of children in school, the children would be speaking with an awareness of the appraisal of their teacher, and might not offer their deeper thoughts. Similarly, if we were to interview children one on one, the children might offer a more careful version of their thoughts to an unknown researcher. What I most wanted was to hear children talking freely, without restraint, in the safety of a place they knew. Therefore I set out to enlist the help of parents, more specifically parents who wanted to tell Bible stories to their children and who would be able to pass on their findings to us.

In the event I published adverts in various national and religious newspapers and magazines inviting people who told stories to children to write in and be part of the research project. After a simple screening process, I sent them 21 stories from the Bible categorized into seven genres. Each parent agreed to record the conversations that followed from reading their child or children a story from each of the seven genres.

What they recorded is what I offer you in this book.

Note: The version of the Bible used in this book is the New Revised Standard Version (NRSV), which is both scholarly and accurate (the RSV being that, commonly used by theological academics)/ I have avoided the use of a child's abridged version as I feel this is likely to become a rapidly outdated version and also be deemed childish (see discussion on this later in the book).

Chapter 1

Texts of Wonder

The Creation (Genesis 1–2 v 3)

(Genesis 1) In the beginning when God created the heavens and the earth, 2 the earth was a formless void and darkness covered the face of the deep, while a wind from God swept over the face of the waters. 3 Then God said, "Let there be light"; and there was light. 4 And God saw that the light was good; and God separated the light from the darkness. 5 God called the light Day, and the darkness he called Night. And there was evening and there was morning, the first day. 6 And God said, "Let there be a dome in the midst of the waters, and let it separate the waters from the waters." 7 So God made the dome and separated the waters that were under the dome from the waters that were above the dome. And it was so. 8 God called the dome Sky. And there was evening and there was morning, the second day. 9 And God said, "Let the waters under the sky be gathered together into one place, and let the dry land appear." And it was so. 10 God called the dry land Earth, and the waters that were gathered together he called Seas. And God saw that it was good. 11 Then God said, "Let the earth put forth vegetation: plants yielding seed, and fruit trees of every kind on earth that bear fruit with the seed in it." And it was so. 12 The earth brought forth vegetation: plants yielding seed of every kind, and trees of every kind bearing fruit with the seed in it. And God saw that it was good. 13 And there was evening and there was morning, the third day. 14 And God said, "Let there be lights in the dome of the sky to separate the day from the night; and let them be for signs and for seasons and for days and years, 15 and let them be lights in the dome of the sky to give light upon the earth." And it was so. 16 God made the two great lights – the greater light to rule the day and the lesser light to rule the night – and the stars. 17 God set them in the dome of the sky to give light upon the earth, 18 to rule over the day and over the night, and to separate the light from the darkness. And God saw that it was good. 19 And there was evening and there was morning, the fourth day. 20 And God said, "Let the waters bring forth swarms of living creatures, and let birds fly above the earth across the dome of the sky." 21 So God created the great sea monsters and every living creature that moves, of every kind, with which the waters swarm, and every winged bird of every kind. And God saw that it was good. 22 God blessed them, saying, "Be fruitful and multiply and fill the waters in the seas, and let birds multiply on the earth." 23 And there was evening and there was morning, the fifth day. 24 And God said, "Let the earth bring forth living creatures of every kind: cattle and creeping things and wild animals of the earth of every kind." And it was so. 25 God made the wild animals of the earth of every kind, and the cattle of every kind, and everything that creeps upon the ground of every kind. And God saw that it was good. 26 Then God said, "Let us make human-kind in our image, according to our likeness; and let them have dominion over the fish of the sea, and over the birds of the air, and over the cattle, and over all the wild animals of the earth, and over every creeping thing that creeps upon the earth." 27 So God created humankind in his image, in the image of God he created them; male and female he created them. 28 God blessed them, and God said to them, "Be fruitful and multiply, and fill the earth and subdue it; and have dominion over the fish of the sea and over the birds of the air and over every living thing that moves upon the earth." 29 God said, "See, I have given you every plant yielding seed that is upon the face of all the earth, and every tree with seed in its fruit; you shall have them for food. 30 And to every beast of the earth, and to every bird of the air, and to everything that creeps on the earth, everything that has the breath of life, I have given every green plant for food." And it was so. 31 God saw everything that he had made, and indeed, it was very good. And there was evening and there was morning, the sixth day.

(Genesis 2) Thus the heavens and the earth were finished, and all their multitude. 2 And on the seventh day God finished the work that he had done, and he rested on the seventh day from all the work that he had done. 3 So God blessed the seventh day and hallowed it, because on it God rested from all the work that he had done in creation.

The Creation (Story 1): The Guiness advert

CONTEXT

This story was told by a father (F) to two teenage sons aged 17 (A) and 14 (B).

DISCUSSION

After the initial reading of that story A wanted some technical clarifications, namely wondering what the dome was in verse 6. He was told that it reflected an early worldview in which the waters above the world were held in a dome supported by pillars. He asked if he had heard correctly that in verse 26 there is a plurality in the Godhead, i.e. *"Let us make mankind in our image."* When he was clear that the verb was plural, he wanted to know if the creation of mankind was male, or male and female reflecting the various genders in the Godhead.

The discussion then developed with further reflection.

A I wonder how humans bred initially. If we take this story literally we have to believe in inter-breeding. Maybe God made more humans in the first place than are recorded here.

F Possibly.

A In fact the whole story might be figurative and be intended to be understood as such. Actually, I guess most of these stories were handed down orally before they were written.

F Yes, I believe you're right.

A (Warming to the theme) I heard it said somewhere that the Hebrew word for "day" is "yom" and it can also be translated as "period". If this is so, then each day of creation can be a period of time.

F Yes. That makes sense. It offers a rational approach.

A But that might cause us problems because by rationalizing the story we're not treating it properly. This story is more like a poem and needs to be allowed to remain like a poem ... so by saying "yom" means "period" I'm becoming overly literal.

F I like that. So, what do you like about this story?

A The first two lines are the best. They have a great poetic picture of God "moving over the face of the waters." It offers the idea of God brooding over the waves of chaos... alien and exciting. He is bringing order and it comes as a sort of development following the hierarchy of nature ending up in humans.
Obviously that is an anthropological perspective.

B It reminds me of the Guinness advert (an advert showing three men in a pub drinking Guinness as the world spins back in time, showing them as cave men, then as Neanderthals and finally as lizards emerging from the swamp).

A Yes. It's a cool story that takes you back to basics. First there is light and darkness. then there is the separation of waters and that is separated from the land.
It's better than the next story in Genesis where women are shown to grow out of men.

B There's another story this reminds me of. You know that Narnia story before the Lion, the Witch and the Wardrobe? It's the one where Narnia is made way back in time for the sons and daughters of Eve.

EXPERIENCES

The father's experience in this conversation was to feel pulled in two directions at once. He felt that his older son was wanting to have an analytical discussion about theology, the Hebrew text and the nature of language. It was a chance for him to demonstrate some of his recent learning and to grapple with his father who was a theologian, but the father felt mindful of his younger son whom he thought might feel left out from the technical conversation.

Fortunately, the conversation redeemed itself for the father by the younger son finding his own way back in by way of anecdotes (the Guinness advert or the Narnia Chronicles).

COMMENT

The point of convergence in this transcript is the common understanding that the creation story is a form of poetic narrative. The two boys, separated by a few key years of secondary education find commonality with each other (and their father) by talking about it in terms of story. The precise interpretation of Hebrew language or the interweaving of the J and P sources in Genesis has its place, but the older son is correct when he says, "by rationalizing the story, we're not treating it properly." (The J and P sources are two of the sources on which the Genesis narrative is based: J the original Jahwist source and P is the later Priestly source.)

These words carry a deep wisdom which many academics would do well to consider in that stories must be understood within their genre. Much of the fundamentalist debate over the literal six-day creation would have been avoided if the simple hermeneutic were applied that "this story is more like a poem and needs to be allowed to remain like a poem."

Interestingly, this realization is also what plays the younger son into the conversation. He is able to contribute in a non-technical way and his contribution has huge validity. This is a reminder that stories can be heard at different developmental and psychological levels, if they are allowed to resonate and are not trapped in specific meaning.

The Creation (Story 2): When God thought it was good

CONTEXT

This story was told by a mother (M) to a daughter (D) aged 7.

DISCUSSION

The telling of this lengthy creation account was punctuated by the child's reactions.

M Tonight we are going to read the story of creation.

D Oh good. I like that story.

D (At v 13) Why does it keep saying, "And God saw it was good?" Why can't it say something like, "God *thought* it was good" or something else?

D (At v 26) I thought it said, "Let us make people, like us but human."

M Yes, but that's a different version of the Bible that we sometimes use. I think you are thinking of "The Street Bible".

D (At v 31) Ah, that's better. It said, "God saw it was very good." It might have said "really good" when the animals were made and "very good" for humans.

D (At 2 v 3 where it talks about God resting). I don't know why we rest on Sundays and go to Church because that is not the seventh day, is it?"

M No, but Jews go to synagogues to worship God on Saturdays which is the seventh day. Christians worship God on Sundays which is the first day of the week in order to be different from Jews. We do this because Jesus rose from the dead on a Sunday.

D Jesus was a Jew.

M Yes and Jesus would have gone to the synagogue on a Saturday.

EXPERIENCE

The mother enjoyed the telling of this story because it engaged her memories of a Christian conference in which she had looked at the creation narrative in some detail.

She was also pleased to notice her daughter's interest in the story and was particularly impressed by her ability to remember the precise wording of a different version (The Street Bible) from a story told several months previously.

COMMENT

The discussion shows the detailed attention that the seven-year-old child has given to the precise wording of the story. Not only can she remember where it departs from a more familiar version, but she is able to suggest ways in which the original writer could have improved the telling.

This amusing commentary on the text shows the girl's complete engagement with the story. Maybe we are hearing something of the way her primary school teacher is helping her to improve her written expressions.

The child's suggestions are in fact most apt and offer the adult new and forgotten dimensions. For example, is it not a rich idea to say that God "thought that" (i.e. had the impression that) his creation was good as opposed to saying that God "saw that" (i.e. pronounced that) his creation was good?

Similarly the little girl wishes God to comment particularly on the creation of animals as well as on humans. This valuing of animals is not only child-like but holds an important sense of ethical value that needs to be heard.

The Creation (Story 3): When there were no houses

CONTEXT

This story was told by a mother (M) and a daughter (D) aged 5.

DISCUSSION

D (Interrupting reading in v 1) What does it mean "formless void?"

M It means nothing was there at all.

D You mean there were no houses or shops?

M Exactly.

D ...and no park...and no hotels?

M No. Nothing existed at all.

D (Interrupting reading at v 6) How did God make a dome in the sky?

M God is very clever.

D (At the end of the reading, commenting on 2 v 3) When it says God hallowed the seventh day and rested, this is like what we do on Sundays.

M Well done Sophie. This is why we have a different day on Sunday.

D How is Sunday different? Is it because of Church?

M I guess that is part of it. Do you think we can make other days of the week "hallowed" too?

D Yes. Every day. God is everywhere all the time.

M So he's here now too?

D Yes.

EXPERIENCE

The mother felt "pleasantly surprised" at the connections being made between Church and Sundays arising from this story. She also enjoyed the conversation as it moved on to approaching God at anytime and in all places. She felt it became a spiritually enriching conversation about bedtime prayers.

COMMENT

This conversation records a five-year-old trying hard to grasp the concept of space and latching onto literal objects as a way of doing so. The mother commented wisely that she felt it important for her daughter to be aware of the fact that she had no concrete answers to many of her questions. She did this whilst also demonstrating her interest in the conversation.

The mother recorded, "The first ten verses were the more difficult to explain but when we got onto reading about vegetation and creatures, she seemed to accept these verses more easily. This may have been due to her personality as she has quite an organized way of thinking and working things out."

This observation is true of many five-year-olds as they endeavour to work out actuality from make-believe and so become experts in wonder. Something of the richness of this process is captured here as the child tests her evolving constructs on her mother, grappling to understand the notion of "nothingness."

The Creation (Story 4): The creation of a hedgehog

CONTEXT

This story was told by a father (F) to a son aged 7 (A) and a son aged 4 (B).

DISCUSSION AND EXPERIENCE

The following notes were offered by the father, interlacing his experience with the tone of the conversation following the reading of the text.

F I wondered how to deal with the nature of truth in this story. I believe in it as a metaphorical truth or myth, but not in a literal sense. I did not want to convey the idea that I really believed this was literally true, only to have to unpick that when the boys are older. But of course they are too young now to understand the difference between metaphorical and literal truth. In the end I chose simply to tell the story without commenting on that aspect, but I was not entirely comfortable with this. The biggest problem was the idea of the "dome". With B I simply changed the idea to "sky". A is interested in space, and so the idea of a dome of water wouldn't make sense to him, so I read the text as it stood and explained that that was what people thought in the old days.

B (younger son) listened carefully to the story without comment. I tried to act it out with voice/hand gestures when appropriate to make it more interesting. I also asked him during the story what he thought the darkness/light/dry land, etc. should be called, and he tried to answer. Afterwards I asked him what animal he would like to have made. He surprised me by saying "hedgehog", but then I remembered that he had plans to make a hedgehog out of an orange and cocktail sticks spiked with cheese for his forthcoming party!

A (older son) was interested in the story at first, but got bored. This was the first time I had simply read it, but it could also be that he was rather tired. He commented when "evening and morning" were repeated, and I then emphasized the pattern of the story, asking him to join in by predicting what I was saying. He enjoyed this at first, but soon resorted to giving silly nonsensical answers. At the end I talked about Sundays and why we keep them special, and he said that they had learnt about that when they had done the creation story at school, which was about nine months ago, I think.

COMMENT

The father's experience details how his own angst about what is literal and what is metaphorical, made the telling of the story difficult. However, his conclusion was to simply read the text as it stands.

This is a wise option as it allows the story to be heard and for the listener to engage with the story – not with the teller's belief system. The older son here will be operating with a "mythical literal worldview" – a world that has non-permanent (and mythical) objects interacting with permanent (and real) objects. Here we see him testing reality, trying to work out what is scientifically accurate and what is the property of narrative. He probably picks up on some of his father's uncertainties in that he gets bored and then becomes silly.

The younger son here will be living in an even more magical world where the legendary and mythical will rub shoulders with the factual.

His attempt to make sense of this is seen when he seizes the idea of God making a hedgehog – something he is currently planning.

The way in which a story can be understood at different levels of meaning and at different levels of literalism is part of the power of ancient narrative. Certainly it is what allows a wide religion to include both those who are poetically liberal and the legally accurate in that they hear the same story but have completely different conclusions.

Moses and the Burning Bush (Exodus 3–4 v 5)

(Exodus 3) Moses was keeping the flock of his father-in-law Jethro, the priest of Midian; he led his flock beyond the wilderness, and came to Horeb, the mountain of God. 2 There the angel of the LORD appeared to him in a flame of fire out of a bush; he looked, and the bush was blazing, yet it was not consumed. 3 Then Moses said, "I must turn aside and look at this great sight, and see why the bush is not burned up." 4 When the LORD saw that he had turned aside to see, God called to him out of the bush, "Moses, Moses!" And he said, "Here I am." 5 Then he said, "Come no closer! Remove the sandals from your feet, for the place on which you are standing is holy ground." 6 He said further, "I am the God of your father, the God of Abraham, the God of Isaac, and the God of Jacob." And Moses hid his face, for he was afraid to look at God. 7 Then the LORD said, "I have observed the misery of my people who are in Egypt; I have heard their cry on account of their taskmasters. Indeed, I know their sufferings, 8 and I have come down to deliver them from the Egyptians, and to bring them up out of that land to a good and broad land, a land flowing with milk and honey, to the country of the Canaanites, the Hittites, the Amorites, the Perizzites, the Hivites, and the Jebusites. 9 The cry of the Israelites has now come to me; I have also seen how the Egyptians oppress them. 10 So come, I will send you to Pharaoh to bring my people, the Israelites, out of Egypt." 11 But Moses said to God, "Who am I that I should go to Pharaoh, and bring the Israelites out of Egypt?" 12 He said, "I will be with you; and this shall be the sign for you that it is I who sent you: when you have brought the people out of Egypt, you shall worship God on this mountain." 13 But Moses said to God, "If I come to the Israelites and say to them, 'The God of your ancestors has sent me to you,' and they ask me, 'What is his name?' what shall I say to them?" 14 God said to Moses, "I AM WHO I AM." He said further, "Thus you shall say to the Israelites, 'I AM has sent me to you.'" 15 God also said to Moses, "Thus you shall say to the Israelites, 'The LORD, the God of your ancestors, the God of Abraham, the God of Isaac, and the God of Jacob, has sent me to you': This is my name forever, and this my title for all generations. 16 Go and assemble the elders of Israel, and say to them, 'The LORD, the God of your ancestors, the God of Abraham, of Isaac, and of Jacob, has appeared to me, saying: I have given heed to you and to what has been done to you in Egypt. 17 I declare that I will bring you up out of the misery of Egypt, to the land of the Canaanites, the Hittites, the Amorites, the Perizzites, the Hivites, and the Jebusites, a land flowing with milk and honey.' 18 They will listen to your voice; and you and the elders of Israel shall go to the king of Egypt and say to him, 'The LORD, the God of the Hebrews, has met with us; let us now go a three days' journey into the wilderness, so that we may sacrifice to the LORD our God.' 19 I know, however, that the king of Egypt will not let you go unless compelled by a mighty hand. 20 So I will stretch out my hand and strike Egypt with all my wonders that I will perform in it; after that he will let you go. 21 I will bring this people into such favour with the Egyptians that, when you go, you will not go empty-handed; 22 each woman shall ask her neighbour and any woman living in the neighbour's house for jewellery of silver and of gold, and clothing, and you shall put them on your sons and on your daughters; and so you shall plunder the Egyptians."

(Exodus 4) Then Moses answered, "But suppose they do not believe me or listen to me, but say, 'The LORD did not appear to you.'" 2 The LORD said to him, "What is that in your hand?" He said, "A staff." 3 And he said, "Throw it on the ground." So he threw the staff on the ground, and it became a snake; and Moses drew back from it. 4 Then the LORD said to Moses, "Reach out your hand, and seize it by the tail" – so he reached out his hand and grasped it, and it became a staff in his hand – 5 "so that they may believe that the LORD, the God of their ancestors, the God of Abraham, the God of Isaac, and the God of Jacob, has appeared to you."

Moses and the Burning Bush (Story 1): When Jesus became a bush

CONTEXT

This story was told by a mother (M) to a son (S) aged 5.

DISCUSSION

M Our story tonight is called "Moses and the Burning Bush".

S I know that one. It's about Jesus becoming a bush and talking to Moses.

M OK. Let's start.

(READS story, interrupted at various points by S to find out whereabouts in the story and place on the page).

S I like that story.

M What do you like about the story?

S I don't know. I can't remember what it's about but I like it.

EXPERIENCE

The mother found this story telling to be an easy experience because her son was well engaged with the process – in keeping with his normal behaviour. She thought it funny that he was unable to actually remember the story.

COMMENT

This brief insight into the process of telling a story is a good example of a child enjoying the event though not necessarily engaging cognitively with the story, even though it was familiar. Wider research shows that the long-term nurture of a child into a faith is serviced well by the ritual of story telling and the gradual deeper acquaintance with stories previously known, even if understanding or meaning is not accessed by the child. Fowler's developmental theory (Fowler 1981) suggests that the meaning of the story is not likely to be available to the child until a later stage (aged 11 upwards).

b) Moses and the Burning Bush (Story 2): The lucky dip

CONTEXT

This story was told by a mother (M) to a son aged 10 (S) and a daughter aged 8 (D).

DISCUSSION

S I know that story.

D Why did God pick Moses out of all the other people? Did he do a lucky dip?

M Maybe.

S I think Moses was surprised … frightened actually when he saw the bush burning but not burning up.

D Yes. He would be shocked… Then when it spoke he must have thought, "why me?"

M Why do you think God told Moses to throw the stick on the floor?

S So that people would believe him when it became a snake.

D No one else could do that. God can do anything.

EXPERIENCE

On an evening when time was limited, this story telling was enjoyable. The mother was amused by her daughter's idea of a lucky dip.

COMMENT

The notion of a lucky dip is a refreshing addition to the mystery of selection. Quite why Israel was chosen as a special nation has remained a mystery to theologians. Similarly the mechanisms of predestination have caused ecclesiological division. Into this complex theological debate, the child's concept of a lucky dip brings a less serious note that reminds us how little we know of God's working. We are however reminded that, "God can do anything."

Moses and the Burning Bush (Story 3): Not a very good trick

CONTEXT

This story was told by a mother (M) to a daughter (D) aged 10.

DISCUSSION

D That was a really nice story. Later it has a happy ending.

M The happy ending is only for the Israelites, not for the Egyptians.

D Oh yes, the Egyptians get nasty plagues and things.
   Poor Moses has an awful lot to remember in this story.

M Can you remember what he has to say?

D No. Only that God is called "I am who I am" and I am has sent him.

M But God says he'll help him.

D But God only does tricks in this story. That was not a very good trick.
   I don't think other children would be very impressed.

EXPERIENCE

The mother thought that this story contained a lot of repetition and that it would bore her daughter and so was surprised to find her initially appreciating the story.

COMMENT

It is possible that this child thought of the burning bush as a trick because of the other incident in the story, namely the metamorphosis of a stick into a snake. She is unimpressed because for her the magic has gone out of the trick and it is merely a clever action that can be replicated. Wonder is removed when the trick is explained. In this instance the story is losing its power because it is explainable.

Moses and the Burning Bush (Story 4): God's code name

CONTEXT

This story was told by a mother (M) to a son (S) aged 6.

DISCUSSION

This story telling was halted by questions from the child at regular intervals. The questions were mainly asking for explanation though they also offered his own reflection.

S (At v 1) Horeb, what's that?

M It's the name of a mountain like Sca Fell or Skiddaw.

S (At v 3) It's funny that sometimes we have this story and the bush is underneath, sometimes it's on top, sometimes it's on the side. Which is the right way?
(In this he was referring to various depictions of the story on television (e.g. Moses, Prince of Egypt and a Bible animation from the BBC).

M These films do not know that the bush looked like exactly. What they do, is to give the same information about the story, like God telling Moses to take his shoes off or God telling Moses his name. Other things like where the bush was or whether Moses wore flip flops, or had dark hair are not so important. It is these minor details that may be different.

S (At v 7) What's a task master?

M A slave driver, someone who made the Israelites work hard.

S (At v 8) A land flowing with milk and honey. That's what God promised to Joshua as well.

M Yes, that's right. Let's look it up and see. (They do so and confirm the child's perception).

S (At v 14) I am who I am. That's a strange name. Is it like a code, like a spy would have?

M What a good idea. In those days, people had names that showed who they were. For example, James (the boy's name) might be called "quick thinker" because he thinks quickly. God's name shows that God is who he is — a mysterious being who has always been there.

S (At v 20) (commenting on God striking Egypt with all his wonders) He really is powerful isn't he? If I stood up on this bed (standing up) and said, "Hail, come down, come on" do you think we'd see any hail? No – exactly, only God can do that.

S (At v 22) What is plunder?

M It's what the winners get after a battle when a city is taken. The Egyptians had got lots of plunder by winning lots of battles and the Israelites were going to be given it by the Egyptians to make them rich.

S (At 4 v 3) God making a staff become a snake shows that he is really powerful. Like if I said to someone I was going to throw my stick down, it wouldn't turn into a snake. Only God can make that happen, only if He was helping me.

EXPERIENCE

The mother noted how animated and excited her son was throughout this story, especially considering that this was a long text, without pictures or animation and that the boy tended to be put off by reading and writing. She wondered if the fact that this was a research project stimulated him.

COMMENT

This story is beloved by children, despite its length and complexity, because at heart there is a surprising and magical revelation. God speaks from a bush and God allows Moses to conjure a snake from a stick. This fact is well known by the film makers and storytellers who have also kept the story alive in other forms.

In this instance, the boy is confident in his role as questioner and the mother responds to his cue as being the one who knows the answer. However, from time to time, he changes tack and comments from his wider knowledge and imagination.

Interestingly, the mother is better at affirming his factual knowledge (e.g. checking elsewhere in the Bible to where God promises Joshua a land flowing with milk and honey) than in encouraging his imagination. His idea of God's name (I am who I am) being "like a code that a spy would have" is a particularly rich reflection.

The Birth of Jesus (Luke 1 v 26–55 & 2 v 1–35)

(Luke 1) 26 In the sixth month the angel Gabriel was sent by God to a town in Galilee called Nazareth, 27 to a virgin engaged to a man whose name was Joseph, of the house of David. The virgin's name was Mary. 28 And he came to her and said, "Greetings, favoured one! The Lord is with you." 29 But she was much perplexed by his words and pondered what sort of greeting this might be. 30 The angel said to her, "Do not be afraid, Mary, for you have found favour with God. 31 And now, you will conceive in your womb and bear a son, and you will name him Jesus. 32 He will be great, and will be called the Son of the Most High, and the Lord God will give to him the throne of his ancestor David. 33 He will reign over the house of Jacob forever, and of his kingdom there will be no end." 34 Mary said to the angel, "How can this be, since I am a virgin?" 35 The angel said to her, "The Holy Spirit will come upon you, and the power of the Most High will overshadow you; therefore the child to be born will be holy; he will be called Son of God. 36 And now, your relative Elizabeth in her old age has also conceived a son; and this is the sixth month for her who was said to be barren. 37 For nothing will be impossible with God." 38 Then Mary said, "Here am I, the servant of the Lord; let it be with me according to your word." Then the angel departed from her. 39 In those days Mary set out and went with haste to a Judean town in the hill country, 40 where she entered the house of Zechariah and greeted Elizabeth. 41 When Elizabeth heard Mary's greeting, the child leaped in her womb. And Elizabeth was filled with the Holy Spirit 42 and exclaimed with a loud cry, "Blessed are you among women, and blessed is the fruit of your womb. 43 And why has this happened to me, that the mother of my Lord comes to me? 44 For as soon as I heard the sound of your greeting, the child in my womb leaped for joy. 45 And blessed is she who believed that there would be a fulfilment of what was spoken to her by the Lord." 46 And Mary said, "My soul magnifies the Lord, 47 and my spirit rejoices in God my Saviour, 48 for he has looked with favour on the lowliness of his servant. Surely, from now on all generations will call me blessed; 49 for the Mighty One has done great things for me, and holy is his name. 50 His mercy is for those who fear him from generation to generation. 51 He has shown strength with his arm; he has scattered the proud in the thoughts of their hearts. 52 He has brought down the powerful from their thrones, and lifted up the lowly; 53 he has filled the hungry with good things, and sent the rich away empty. 54 He has helped his servant Israel, in remembrance of his mercy, 55 according to the promise he made to our ancestors, to Abraham and to his descendants forever."

(Luke 2) In those days a decree went out from Emperor Augustus that all the world should be registered. 2 This was the first registration and was taken while Quirinius was governor of Syria. 3 All went to their own towns to be registered. 4 Joseph also went from the town of Nazareth in Galilee to Judea, to the city of David called Bethlehem, because he was descended from the house and family of David. 5 He went to be registered with Mary, to whom he was engaged and who was expecting a child. 6 While they were there, the time came for her to deliver her child. 7 And she gave birth to her firstborn son and wrapped him in bands of cloth, and laid him in a manger, because there was no place for them in the inn. 8 In that region there were shepherds living in the fields, keeping watch over their flock by night. 9 Then an angel of the Lord stood before them, and the glory of the Lord shone around them, and they were terrified. 10 But the angel said to them, "Do not be afraid; for see – I am bringing you good news of great joy for all the people: 11 to you is born this day in the city of David a Saviour, who is the Messiah, the Lord. 12 This will be a sign for you: you will find a child wrapped in bands of cloth and lying in a manger." 13 And suddenly there was with the angel a multitude of the heavenly host, praising God and saying, 14 "Glory to God in the highest heaven, and on earth peace among those whom he favours!" 15 When the angels had left them and gone into heaven, the shepherds said to one another, "Let us go now to Bethlehem and see this thing that has taken place, which the Lord has made known to us." 16 So they went with haste and found Mary and Joseph, and the child lying in the manger. 17 When they saw this, they made known what had been told them about this child; 18 and all who heard it were amazed at what the shepherds told them. 19 But Mary treasured all these words and pondered them in her heart. 20 The shepherds returned, glorifying and praising God for all they had heard and seen, as it had been told them. 21 After eight days had passed, it was time to circumcise the child; and he was called Jesus, the name given by the angel before he was conceived in the womb. 22 When the time came for their purification according to the law of Moses, they brought him up to

Jerusalem to present him to the Lord 23 (as it is written in the law of the Lord, "Every firstborn male shall be designated as holy to the Lord"), 24 and they offered a sacrifice according to what is stated in the law of the Lord, "a pair of turtledoves or two young pigeons." 25 Now there was a man in Jerusalem whose name was Simeon; this man was righteous and devout, looking forward to the consolation of Israel, and the Holy Spirit rested on him. 26 It had been revealed to him by the Holy Spirit that he would not see death before he had seen the Lord's Messiah. 27 Guided by the Spirit, Simeon came into the temple; and when the parents brought in the child Jesus, to do for him what was customary under the law, 28 Simeon took him in his arms and praised God, saying, 29 "Master, now you are dismissing your servant in peace, according to your word; 30 for my eyes have seen your salvation, 31 which you have prepared in the presence of all peoples, 32 a light for revelation to the Gentiles and for glory to your people Israel." 33 And the child's father and mother were amazed at what was being said about him. 34 Then Simeon blessed them and said to his mother Mary, "This child is destined for the falling and the rising of many in Israel, and to be a sign that will be opposed 35 so that the inner thoughts of many will be revealed – and a sword will pierce your own soul too."

The Birth of Jesus (Story 1): This is an advert

CONTEXT

This story was told by a father (F) to two teenage sons aged 17 (A) and 14 (B).

DISCUSSION

B Why didn't Jesus have any brothers?

A He did. It's just that he was the first born and it's Him everyone talks about. This was written by Luke a long time after Jesus was born. It was written after he had died, as an advert for the early Church!

B Isn't this story shorter than the other ones (gospels) about Jesus' birth?

A No, it's just different. It's an advert because it's showing how special Jesus was after he was born. It's trying to say He was the Son of God. The story is a re-telling but it's got the basis of truth.

F What do you mean?

A Well, take Mary's words for example. Here is a very young Jewish woman coming out with the wise words of the Magnificat. How could she have said these words? She might not even have understood them if she was only 14 years old.

F So what do you think happened in this story.

A I'm told that the Hebrew word for "virgin" can also mean "young woman." So… Mary might not necessarily have been a virgin as we understand it. Therefore Jesus could be the seed of a man.

B That's all very clever but clarify. Are you saying that Joseph was Jesus' Dad?
(Conversation became very animated and feisty with the sexual encounter discussed by two teenage boys, the older of whom suggested it could have been Joseph or even "the angel" who was the actual father rather than the Holy Spirit "overshadowing Mary.")
How can Jesus be God's Son then if he is not actually "God's Son"?

F The Church has always taught that it was Mary's egg and God's seed and so Jesus is both human and divine.

A Why does this birth have to be so supernatural? Are not all natural births somehow supernatural?

B I don't know why this story does not make use of Joseph.

A It does in another gospel where Joseph becomes dumb. But it's true, the gospels don't mention Joseph much at all. They're only interested in making Jesus divine.

B Well, can't God do anything?

A Maybe He can, but does he?

B Well if he made the world, can't he make a baby?

A Yes, but he could do it as a normal birth too. Normal birth is wondrous.

B So do you believe that there are any miracles and magical stuff in the Bible?

A I believe in the resurrection.

EXPERIENCE

The father recorded this wide-ranging conversation with difficulty and sensed it showed two very different perspectives. They each wanted something different from the story. His older son wanted to rationalize the birth narrative and the younger son wanted to accept it more traditionally.

COMMENT

This recorded encounter shows two stages of development. The younger boy is at Fowler's stage three of faith development (called "synthetic conventional") – a stage when faith endeavours to fit in with the wider corpus of tradition. This is a more tribal position in which it is important to identify the laws of authority and to have a right way of believing. Therefore the 14-year-old appeals to theology whereby Jesus is God's Son and whereby God can do anything. He only allows his older brother off the hook when he says something more orthodox (i.e. I believe in the resurrection).

The older boy is moving into stage four of Fowler's faith stage development (called "individuative reflective") – a stage when faith forms an individual stance away from the tribe, and is worked out more reflectively as the individual fits the story into other worldviews.

The father's role is more ambiguous in that he endeavours to get the older boy to clarify his thinking, but also offers the traditional orthodoxy of the Church. In this his role is to protect the younger son but also to take the older son seriously. As such he plays an invaluable role of allowing theological reflection between the two boys.

Interestingly it is the younger son (the more orthodox believer) who asks the open and reflective questions whereas it is the older son (the more liberal thinker) who pronounces his new truths emphatically.

Chapter 2

Texts of Adventure and Leadership

David and the Mighty Men (2 Samuel 23 v 13–17)

(2 Samuel 23) 13 Towards the beginning of harvest three of the thirty chiefs went down to join David at the cave of Adullam, while a band of Philistines was encamped in the valley of Rephaim. 14 David was then in the stronghold; and the garrison of the Philistines was then at Bethlehem. 15 David said longingly, "O that someone would give me water to drink from the well of Bethlehem that is by the gate!" 16 Then the three warriors broke

through the camp of the Philistines, drew water from the well of Bethlehem that was by the gate, and brought it to David. But he would not drink of it; he poured it out to the LORD, 17 for he said, "The LORD forbid that I should do this. Can I drink the blood of the men who went at the risk of their lives?" Therefore he would not drink it. The three warriors did these things.

David and the Mighty Men (Story 1): Drinking the blood of men

CONTEXT

This story was told by a mother (M) to a son (S) aged 5.

DISCUSSION

S I like this story. It's not a long one. Can I read it myself? (reads story).

Why did David live in a cave? Did his father and mother not look after him?

M David was grown up by the time of this story.

S What were his father and mother called?

M We don't know this information.

S Why did David not drink the water that his warriors brought him?

M He poured it out as a present for God. Because his warriors had risked their lives to bring him the water, he thought it was very precious water and would make a good present for God.

EXPERIENCE

The mother was intrigued at the level of engagement that her son had with this story, listening very intently and even reading it through himself.

As she read the story first time and read the words on David's lips, "Can I drink the blood of the men who went at the risk of their lives?", her son loudly exclaimed "Yes!"

COMMENT

The engagement of a five-year-old boy with this text is quite startling. This will be partly due to the subject matter of mighty men and partly due to his current acquisition of reading skills (in which he is advanced). The text is short enough for him to read through himself and so to allow him to digest more thoroughly.

His outburst at the end to state his belief that David should drink the blood of his men shows his full identification with the story. However, it is surprising in that the small boy is likely to have a literalist understanding of the question being posed, in other words to believe that David was actually asking whether or not he could drink blood.

David and the Mighty Men (Story 2): A waste of water

CONTEXT

This story was told by a father (F) to a son aged 10 (S) and a daughter aged 8 (D).

DISCUSSION

F So what did you think of this story?

D I think that David was teasing his three men a little.

S He put them at risk. Maybe this was because they were so loyal.

F Maybe.

S Did David break a commandment by wanting something that wasn't his?

F Interesting idea, but I don't think so.

D I think it was a waste of water.

EXPERIENCE

This was a fairly straightforward story telling occasion.

COMMENT

The children offer some ideas that are certainly worthy of further reflection in that they open up new avenues of thought and which evidence the fact that they are at a lower place in the hierarchic order. One of these is the possibility that David is teasing his men – teasing being a part of life for most children as they discover humour and engage in more sophisticated reality testing. Another idea is that David is wasting the water, wasting being a sin against which many children are trained.

The Fall of Jericho (Joshua 2 v 1–24 & 6 v 1–27)

(Joshua 2) Then Joshua son of Nun sent two men secretly from Shittim as spies, saying, "Go, view the land, especially Jericho." So they went, and entered the house of a prostitute whose name was Rahab, and spent the night there. 2 The king of Jericho was told, "Some Israelites have come here tonight to search out the land." 3 Then the king of Jericho sent orders to Rahab, "Bring out the men who have come to you, who entered your house, for they have come only to search out the whole land." 4 But the woman took the two men and hid them. Then she said, "True, the men came to me, but I did not know where they came from. 5 And when it was time to close the gate at dark, the men went out. Where the men went I do not know. Pursue them quickly, for you can overtake them." 6 She had, however, brought them up to the roof and hidden them with the stalks of flax that she had laid out on the roof. 7 So the men pursued them on the way to the Jordan as far as the fords. As soon as the pursuers had gone out, the gate was shut. 8 Before they went to sleep, she came up to them on the roof 9 and said to the men: "I know that the LORD has given you the land, and that dread of you has fallen on us, and that all the inhabitants of the land melt in fear before you. 10 For we have heard how the LORD dried up the water of the Red Sea before you when you came out of Egypt, and what you did to the two kings of the Amorites that were beyond the Jordan, to Sihon and Og, whom you utterly destroyed. 11 As soon as we heard it, our hearts melted, and there was no courage left in any of us because of you. The LORD your God is indeed God in heaven above and on earth below. 12 Now then, since I have dealt kindly with you, swear to me by the LORD that you in turn will deal kindly with my family. Give me a sign of good faith 13 that you will spare my father and mother, my brothers and sisters, and all who belong to them, and deliver our lives from death." 14 The men said to her, "Our life for yours! If you do not tell this business of ours, then we will deal kindly and faithfully with you when the LORD gives us the land." 15 Then she let them down by a rope through the window, for her house was on the outer side of the city wall and she resided within the wall itself. 16 She said to them, "Go toward the hill country, so that the pursuers may not come upon you. Hide yourselves there three days, until the pursuers have returned; then afterward you may go your way." 17 The men said to her, "We will be released from this oath that you have made us swear to you 18 if we invade the land and you do not tie this crimson cord in the window through which you let us down, and you do not gather into your house your father and mother, your brothers, and all your family. 19 If any of you go out of the doors of your house into the street, they shall be responsible for their own death, and we shall be innocent; but if a hand is laid upon any who are with you in the house, we shall bear the responsibility for their death. 20 But if you tell this business of ours, then we shall be released from this oath that you made us swear to you." 21 She said, "According to your words, so be it." She sent them away and they departed. Then she tied the crimson cord in the window. 22 They departed and went into the hill country and stayed there three days, until the pursuers returned. The pursuers had searched all along the way and found nothing. 23 Then the two men came down again from the hill country. They crossed over, came to Joshua son of Nun, and told him all that had happened to them. 24 They said to Joshua, "Truly the LORD has given all the land into our hands; moreover all the inhabitants of the land melt in fear before us."

(Joshua 6) Now Jericho was shut up inside and out because of the Israelites; no one came out and no one went in. 2 The LORD said to Joshua, "See, I have handed Jericho over to you, along with its king and soldiers. 3 You shall march around the city, all the warriors circling the city once. Thus you shall do for six days, 4 with seven priests bearing seven trumpets of rams' horns before the ark. On the seventh day you shall march around the city seven times, the priests blowing the trumpets. 5 When they make a long blast with the ram's horn, as soon as you hear the sound of the trumpet, then all the people shall shout with a great shout; and the wall of the city will fall down flat, and all the people shall charge straight ahead." 6 So Joshua son of Nun summoned the priests and said to them, "Take up the ark of the covenant, and have seven priests carry seven trumpets of rams' horns in front of the ark of the LORD." 7 To the people he said, "Go forward and march around the city; have the armed men pass on before the ark of the LORD." 8 As Joshua had commanded the people, the seven priests carrying the seven trumpets of rams' horns before the LORD went forward, blowing the trumpets, with the ark of the covenant of the LORD following them. 9 And the armed men went before the priests who blew the trumpets; the rear guard came after the ark, while the trumpets blew continually. 10 To the people Joshua gave this command: "You shall not shout or let your voice be heard, nor shall you utter a word, until the day I tell you to shout. Then you shall shout." 11 So the ark of the LORD went around the city, circling it once; and they came into the camp, and spent the night in the camp. 12 Then Joshua rose early in the morning, and the priests took up the ark of the LORD. 13 The seven priests carrying the seven trumpets of rams' horns before the ark of the LORD passed on, blowing the trumpets continually. The armed men went before them, and the rear guard came after the ark of the LORD, while the trumpets blew continually. 14 On the second day they marched around the city once and then returned to the camp. They did this for six days. 15 On the seventh day they rose early, at dawn, and marched around the city in the same manner seven times. It was only on that day that they marched around the city seven times. 16 And at the seventh time, when the priests had blown the trumpets, Joshua said to the people, "Shout! For the LORD has given you the city. 17 The city and all that is in it shall be devoted to the LORD for destruction. Only Rahab the prostitute and all who are with her in her house shall live because she hid the messengers we sent. 18 As for you, keep away from the things devoted to destruction, so as not to covet and take any of the devoted things and make the camp of Israel an object for destruction, bringing trouble upon it. 19 But all silver and gold, and vessels of bronze and iron, are sacred to the LORD; they shall go into the treasury of the LORD." 20 So the people shouted, and the trumpets were blown. As soon as the people heard the sound of the trumpets, they raised a great shout, and the wall fell down flat; so the people charged straight ahead into the city and captured it. 21 Then they devoted to destruction by the edge of the sword all in the city, both men and women, young and old, oxen, sheep, and donkeys. 22 Joshua said to the two men who had spied out the land, "Go into the prostitute's house, and bring the woman out of it and all who belong to her, as you swore to her." 23 So the young men who had been spies went in and brought Rahab out, along with her father, her mother, her brothers, and all who belonged to her – they brought all her kindred out – and set them outside the camp of Israel. 24 They burned down the city, and everything in it; only the silver and gold, and the vessels of bronze and iron, they put into the treasury of the house of the LORD. 25 But Rahab the prostitute, with her family and all who belonged to her, Joshua spared. Her family has lived in Israel ever since. For she hid the messengers whom Joshua sent to spy out Jericho. 26 Joshua then pronounced this oath, saying, "Cursed before the LORD be anyone who tries to build this city – this Jericho! At the cost of his firstborn he shall lay its foundation, and at the cost of his youngest he shall set up its gates!" 27 So the LORD was with Joshua; and his fame was in all the land.

The Fall of Jericho (Story 1): Why does God kill?

CONTEXT

This story was told by a mother (M) to a daughter (D) aged 7.

DISCUSSION

D I don't like the way that everyone in Jericho had to get killed. Why does this have to happen?

M Well, God had told Joshua to take the city and the land.

D Why did God say it was alright to destroy Jericho?

M I don't think that God actually said it was alright to kill people. God knew that people might die as that is what happens in a war.

D Why did God give this land to the Israelites?

M (Thinking hard)… because long before all this happened the Israelites had lived there before they were taken away as slaves to Egypt.

D Well I still don't think it's fair to take it back by killing everyone.

M This story was written a long time before Jesus was born at a time when people had different ideas about God from us.

D Do you actually think this story is true?

M Well the Bible means "a library" and it holds a lot of books. Some of these books are stories and some are historical accounts.

D OK.

EXPERIENCE

Clearly this discussion shows a mother being hard-pressed by a daughter who is unhappy at the lack of justice being shown in a biblical story.

The mother's pressure had started earlier in the evening when outside events had disrupted domestic arrangements. The mother had ended up having an overly busy evening.

In her notes concerning the discussion, the mother was a little perplexed that her daughter had only focused on the death of the inhabitants of Jericho and not on the leadership of Joshua. She had hoped to have replicated her experiences as a child hearing the story when she had enjoyed banging and trumpeting in a mime of the walls coming down. She wrote, "I think it says something about how children perceive the world today."

COMMENT

The mother is correct that a new generation of children perceive the world differently and this transcript shows the two worlds in striking contrast. It is likely that this mother never fully engaged with the story from an ethical dimension, rather from a more triumphalist perspective in which the spiritual message is the main consideration.

In this encounter, it is the child who wins the engagement by effectively dwelling on the ethical issues and questioning the veracity of the story. Caught on the hop, and feeling that she must defend the story, the mother has to concede that the story (and other ancient biblical texts before Jesus) contained different ideas about God and were less than accurate.

If the mother had felt less defensive, she might have been more able to value her daughter's powerful ethical sense of justice and to affirm it. In the next story, we see an exact role reversal between the child and the mother in a different household.

The Fall of Jericho (Story 2): God is good

CONTEXT

This story was told by a mother (M) to a daughter (D) aged 10.

DISCUSSION

D Nice story.

M What do you mean by that?

D It shows God getting rid of bad people. He only does it because they deserve it. He keeps Rahab because she is good.

M Don't you think it's wrong to destroy all the people in Jericho?

D No. God is good.

(Starts singing song about the battle of Jericho)

EXPERIENCE

The mother found it strange that her daughter was not disturbed by a story in which people get hurt and where God's role is simply to punish bad people and reward good people. She was also surprised that her daughter was so motivated by such a long script. At a later stage she was pleased to hear her daughter recap a huge section of the story.

COMMENT

The child is at a stage of moral reasoning which is concrete and literal and which has no space for ambiguity whereby the clear line of truth must be maintained at all costs. Because she equates God with goodness, she does not question whether or not he is right, quickly excusing Him when challenged by her mother. This is a period of certainty which the child is preserving in order to protect her zone of comfort. Were she to continue to protect her certainty into adulthood, that would cause a moral dilemma in that her reasoning could be used to justify holy wars or to condone almost any action. However, seen in the developing world of a ten-year-old, her insights can be listened to and accepted.

This account makes an interesting contrast to that just described in a different household.

The Fall of Jericho (Story 3): Don't ask what a prostitute is!

CONTEXT

This story was told by a father (F) to a son aged 7 (A) and a son aged 4 (B).

DISCUSSION AND EXPERIENCE

The following notes were offered by the father interlacing his experience with the tone of the conversation following an ad-lib account of the story.

F I enjoyed telling the story, as I was able to make it exciting, and introduce humorous sound effects for the siege scenes (although I wondered whether the original authors would have approved of us finding this humorous!). I was a bit concerned about Rahab, since I didn't want to (and probably couldn't appropriately) explain what a prostitute was! Nevertheless I felt that this meant the children miss an important element of the story, because it helps us understand her actions and her place in the city, as well as potential points about God choosing those on the margins.

B did not want a story from me tonight, but changed his mind when he heard it was to be an "exciting story about soldiers." During the story he commented that "red rope rhymes with Rahab." He did not make any other comment during the story, but listened attentively, and afterwards was able to answer factual questions about the story. However, he did not express any opinions – he simply accepted the story as it stood.

A when told in advance simply that it was to be about "Jericho", without any further hints began to sing the song "Joshua fought the battle of Jericho," which he knows from a children's tape. He also listened attentively, and giggled a lot at the humorous description of the siege. He said that was his favourite part of the story when asked. However, like B, while he could answer factual questions about the story, he didn't express any other opinion.

A had not seen the stories on the coloured sheets from the folder before tonight. I let him look at the end, having explained beforehand that it was important to the researcher's project that I told him the story first before he read it. He was very interested in the way the text was presented. He wanted to know why the story began with "Then…" and what the numbers in the text were all about. This developed into a discussion about the way the Bible is structured into books, of which these stories were only a small part. We got out a proper Bible and found the story. A was amazed that the words were identical! After the story telling session, A wanted to read the text on the sheet himself, despite being warned that he might struggle to understand it. He did then read the whole story to himself. Fortunately he didn't ask what a prostitute was!

COMMENT

This account illustrates the way young boys are fascinated by exciting stories about soldiers. What stands out is the humour of the event, which the father rightly reflects was not a part of the author's intention.

However, removed from its historical and socio-historical context, the fall of Jericho does become the property of action songs and drama – a version of story telling that wants to gag the original story. Indeed, the father finds himself having to suppress the fact that a prostitute is a key character.

Paul's Shipwreck (Acts 27)

Acts 27 When it was decided that we were to sail for Italy, they transferred Paul and some other prisoners to a centurion of the Augustan Cohort, named Julius. 2 Embarking on a ship of Adramyttium that was about to set sail to the ports along the coast of Asia, we put to sea, accompanied by Aristarchus, a Macedonian from Thessalonica. 3 The next day we put in at Sidon; and Julius treated Paul kindly, and allowed him to go to his friends to be cared for. 4 Putting out to sea from there, we sailed under the lee of Cyprus, because the winds were against us. 5 After we had sailed across the sea that is off Cilicia and Pamphylia, we came to Myra in Lycia. 6 There the centurion found an Alexandrian ship bound for Italy and put us on board. 7 We sailed slowly for a number of days and arrived with difficulty off Cnidus, and as the wind was against us, we sailed under the lee of Crete off Salmone. 8 Sailing past it with difficulty, we came to a place called Fair Havens, near the city of Lasea. 9 Since much time had been lost and sailing was now dangerous, because even the Fast had already gone by, Paul advised them, 10 saying, "Sirs, I can see that the voyage will be with danger and much heavy loss, not only of the cargo and the ship, but also of our lives." 11 But the centurion paid more attention to the pilot and to the owner of the ship than to what Paul said. 12 Since the harbour was not suitable for spending the winter, the majority was in favour of putting to sea from there, on the chance that somehow they could reach Phoenix, where they could spend the winter. It was a harbour of Crete, facing southwest and northwest. 13 When a moderate south wind began to blow, they thought they could achieve their purpose; so they weighed anchor and began to sail past Crete, close to the shore. 14 But soon a violent wind, called the northeaster, rushed down from Crete. 15 Since the ship was caught and could not be turned head-on into the wind, we gave way to it and were driven. 16 By running under the lee of a small island called Cauda we were scarcely able to get the ship's boat under control. 17 After hoisting it up they took measures to undergird the ship; then, fearing that they would run on the Syrtis, they lowered the sea anchor and so were driven. 18 We were being pounded by the storm so violently that on the next day they began to throw the cargo overboard, 19 and on the third day with their own hands they threw the ship's tackle overboard. 20 When neither sun nor stars appeared for many days, and no small tempest raged, all hope of our being saved was at last abandoned. 21 Since they had been without food for a long time, Paul then stood up among them and said, "Men, you should have listened to me and not have set sail from Crete and thereby avoided this damage and loss. 22 I urge you now to keep up your courage, for there will be no loss of life among you, but only of the ship. 23 For last night there stood by me an angel of the God to whom I belong and whom I worship, 24 and he said, "Do not be afraid, Paul; you must stand before the emperor; and indeed, God has granted safety to all those who are sailing with you." 25 So keep up your courage, men, for I have faith in God that it will be exactly as I have been told. 26 But we will have to run aground on some island." 27 When the fourteenth night had come, as we were drifting across the sea of Adria, about midnight the sailors suspected that they were nearing land. 28 So they took soundings and found twenty fathoms; a little farther on they took soundings again and found fifteen fathoms. 29 Fearing that we might run on the rocks, they let down four anchors from the stern and prayed for day to come. 30 But when the sailors tried to escape from the ship and had lowered the boat into the sea, on the pretext of putting out anchors from the bow, 31 Paul said to the centurion and the soldiers, "Unless these men stay in the ship, you cannot be saved." 32 Then the soldiers cut away the ropes of the boat and set it adrift. 33 Just before daybreak, Paul urged all of them to take some food, saying, "Today is the fourteenth day that you have been in suspense and remaining without food, having eaten nothing. 34 Therefore I urge you to take some food, for it will help you survive; for none of you will lose a hair from your heads." 35 After he had said this, he took bread; and giving thanks to God in the presence of all, he broke it and began to eat. 36 Then all of them were encouraged and took food for themselves. 37 (We were in all two hundred seventy-six persons in the ship.) 38 After they had satisfied their hunger, they lightened the ship by throwing the wheat into the sea. 39 In the morning they did not recognize the land, but they noticed a bay with a beach, on which they planned to run the ship ashore, if they could. 40 So they cast off the anchors and left them in the sea. At the same time they loosened the ropes that tied the steering-oars; then hoisting the foresail to the wind, they made for the beach. 41 But striking a reef, they ran the ship aground; the bow stuck and remained immovable, but the stern was being broken up by the force of the waves. 42 The soldiers' plan was to kill the prisoners, so that none might swim away and escape; 43 but the centurion, wishing to save Paul, kept them from carrying out their plan. He ordered those who could swim to jump overboard first and make for the land, 44 and the rest to follow, some on planks and others on pieces of the ship. And so it was that all were brought safely to land.

Paul's Shipwreck (Story 1): The ship's log

CONTEXT

This story was told by a father (F) to two teenage sons aged 17 (A) and 14 (B).

DISCUSSION

B In this story the storyteller says "we". Is that because Luke was on board ship with Paul at the time of the shipwreck?

F Yes. Interesting isn't it?

B I'm surprised that the Roman centurion listened to Paul and ordered for the lifeboat to be cut adrift.

A It shows that Paul was respected. By the way, why was Paul going to Rome?

F Because he was due to be tried by a higher court, the court of Caesar. He'd claimed this right as a Roman citizen.

A Was Jesus a Roman citizen?

F Not to my knowledge. He was very much a Jew being brought up in an area of occupation. To become a Roman citizen, if you were not born in Rome, you had to undergo a ceremony.

(Discussion about Jesus and his culture.)

Anyway, back to the story; It's quite interesting.

B So how does Paul finally die when he escapes the shipwreck?

F It is presumed that after Paul got to Rome, he died in prison.

B The centurion is an interesting man…giving food to everyone, then tipping the food into the sea before they even arrive at the land. Was he a Christian?

A Probably not. He just realized that Paul was worth listening to.

By the way it's bizarre that he had to stop his soldiers from killing the prisoners to prevent them from escaping. This is a serious confusion in the soldiers' priorities. I wonder if the prisoners did try to escape… actually I guess there would not be much point trying to escape on a tiny island. Can we see it today?

F Yes. The island is called Gozo, off the coast of Malta.

A This is a cool story. There's so much detail. It has an authentic ring to it as well as the story being interesting. It reads a bit like a ship's log.

EXPERIENCE

The father experienced this discussion with a little frustration since the details that appealed to him as a day skipper (someone who had an off-shore qualification to sail and navigate) were not being noted by his sons.

Also, he felt responsible for keeping a direction to the conversation, which veered largely in other directions – explaining the legal nature of Roman citizenship or the culture of Jesus. He felt that the discussion was not particularly focused or logical and contained considerable imaginative reflection that was outside of his knowledge.

COMMENT

There is a strong sense that this conversation bridges the current factual knowledge of the father and his sons and the wider unknown knowledge of what is sensed when wonder enters the discussion. It is a quality that all storytellers are hoping to produce.

Therefore, although the father is frustrated not to be able to control the conversation or the flow of knowledge (something he and all parents must learn to stand back from), he is part of a process of mutual discovery and learning. This bodes well for future dialogue between the two generations in that the story telling session is showing all participants to be ignorant of the whole picture and therefore equalized as wonderers and learners. It is a reminder that no one owns the story and that all ages can engage with it. Those who learn to wonder together, without appointing a single expert or overall leader, are likely to return to this point of wondering together.

Paul's Shipwreck (Story 2): Not eating for 14 days
CONTEXT

This story was told at a Church Youth Group by a Youth Leader. The group consisted of five self-selected teenagers, four girls aged 13 (A), 13 (B), 13 (C) and 15 (D) and a boy aged 14 (E). They had opted to be in this group because the subject of the story was a "text of adventure".

One of the 13-year-olds (C) and the 15-year-old (D) were sisters. The whole group was white British except for B who was from Pakistan.

DISCUSSION

The transcript for the conversation resulting from the reading of this story is terse, with the youth leader noting that the girls were surprised to find a story of survival from a shipwreck being entitled as an adventure story. They were expecting something that had romance and puzzles. If it was about a shipwreck then they would have expected it to be swash-buckling and to involve events on high ropes and daring exploits.

The conversation continued:

D I would have thought an adventure story would be more fun... not coming within a millimetre of death.

C No. It doesn't sound like fun if you don't eat for 14 days.

E I'm surprised it doesn't give more detail about not eating for 14 days. I wonder how you do that?

A I think it shows God's power though. (Pause) God can do anything he wants to do.

C But if you know God will save you that takes away the fun. I know this story and hearing it again reminds me that Paul knew it would all be OK.

D Yes, but it still seems amazing hearing of storms and running aground. I believe storms still threaten shipping in that area of the Mediterranean today.

B It's good to see that it was a prisoner who saved the day. Normally it's the captain who saves the ship.

E Yes. It reminds me of Treasure Island.

A More like Robinson Crusoe.

B Or "I'm a celebrity, get me out of here!"

EXPERIENCE

The youth leader's experience was to be a little disappointed that the story did not create more interest and was not considered to be very adventurous. She thought that the group were trying very hard to make something of it and did not succeed because their thoughts were so disjointed and because they were trying to accommodate a 14-year-old boy

(E) who did not seem to fit into the wider group, nor into this particular group.

COMMENT

Although the contributions to this discussion were disjointed, they show considerable breadth of reflection and knowledge which could have been developed with encouragement. For example the idea of fasting for 14 days, sailing in adverse weather conditions in the Mediterranean, perceiving God's mind in adversity or simply comparing the story to contemporary stories, are all initiated by the group.

The familiarity with the story has effectively removed some of the power of the sacred text. The notion that because the story shows Paul prophesying that everyone will reach land safely makes the story dull, is a failure to engage with the risk of Paul's venture, or with the complexity of discerning God's mind. As Pike has noted (2003a and b), familiarity with the sacred text can actually become an obstacle to reading the Bible because we offer too much reverence and fail to grapple with the story and its meaning.

In contrast with this is the disappointment that this well-known story is not as swashbuckling as other contemporary tales, which is presumably an acknowledgement that the Biblical texts are not as entertaining nor as accessible to teenagers as current films, TV shows or books. It is however of interest to note the attempts by some group members to add relevance and credibility to the story.

Chapter 3

Texts of Terror

Abraham and Isaac (Genesis 22 v 1–19)

(Genesis 22) After these things God tested Abraham. He said to him, "Abraham!" And he said, "Here I am." 2 He said, "Take your son, your only son Isaac, whom you love, and go to the land of Moriah, and offer him there as a burnt offering on one of the mountains that I shall show you." 3 So Abraham rose early in the morning, saddled his donkey, and took two of his young men with him, and his son Isaac; he cut the wood for the burnt offering, and set out and went to the place in the distance that God had shown him. 4 On the third day Abraham looked up and saw the place far away. 5 Then Abraham said to his young men, "Stay here with the donkey; the boy and I will go over there; we will worship, and then we will come back to you." 6 Abraham took the wood of the burnt offering and laid it on his son Isaac, and he himself carried the fire and the knife. So the two of them walked on together. 7 Isaac said to his father Abraham, "Father!" And he said, "Here I am, my son." He said, "The fire and the wood are here, but where is the lamb for a burnt offering?" 8 Abraham said, "God himself will provide the lamb for a burnt offering, my son." So the two of them walked on together. 9 When they came to the place that God had shown him, Abraham built an altar there and laid the wood in order. He bound his son Isaac, and laid him on the altar, on top of the wood. 10 Then Abraham reached out his hand and took the knife to kill his son. 11 But the angel of the LORD called to him from heaven, and said, "Abraham, Abraham!" And he said, "Here I am." 12 He said, "Do not lay your hand on the boy or do anything to him; for now I know that you fear God, since you have not withheld your son, your only son, from me." 13 And Abraham looked up and saw a ram, caught in a thicket by its horns. Abraham went and took the ram and offered it up as a burnt offering instead of his son. 14 So Abraham called that place "The LORD will provide"; as it is said to this day, "On the mount of the LORD it shall be provided." 15 The angel of the LORD called to Abraham a second time from heaven, 16 and said, "By myself I have sworn, says the LORD: Because you have done this, and have not withheld your son, your only son, 17 I will indeed bless you, and I will make your offspring as numerous as the stars of heaven and as the sand that is on the seashore. And your offspring shall possess the gate of their enemies, 18 and by your offspring shall all the nations of the earth gain blessing for themselves, because you have obeyed my voice." 19 So Abraham returned to his young men, and they arose and went together to Beer-sheba; and Abraham lived at Beer-sheba.

Abraham and Isaac (Story 1): God or Family?

CONTEXT

This story was told at a Church youth group by a youth leader (X). The group consisted of four self-selected teenage lads aged 13 (A), 15 (B), 15 (C) and 18 (D). They had opted to be in this group because the subject of the story was a "text of terror".

The 13-year-old (A) and one of the 15-year-olds (B) were brothers, who had come over to England from Pakistan five years previously. The other 15-year-old was Caucasian, whose mother was a minister in the Church. The 18-year-old was African-Caribbean.

DISCUSSION

After the story was read, the group consensus was that it was "not very terrifying" and that there was "not much suspense." In fact they asked why it was entitled a text of terror since there was no fighting and very little violence. It was at this point that one lad C commented that the story would be terrifying for Isaac.

The conversation continued with A suggesting that the story was simply a test for Abraham to see if he really trusted God. However, there was wider concern that if God was so trustworthy and caring, why did he let Abraham kill the ram?

A That story was not very terrifying.

D No, there was no suspense

B There was no fighting. Why is it called a "text of terror"?

C There was no violence but it would have been terrifying for Isaac.

A I think it was just a test for Abraham and he passed the test.

X Yes, it showed Abraham's trust for God.

C I don't get why if God is so caring and trustworthy, he let Abraham kill the ram.

X (after long pause). Do you think Abraham did the right thing?

A Of course. He showed that he loved God more than his family by being prepared to kill his son.

B Yes. It is right to put God before your family.

C I'm not sure about that. I think Abraham would have felt really guilty if he'd killed Isaac (pause). We know our family better than we know God and I'd rather have my family than God.

A No, your family doesn't matter. If you lost your family, God would look after you. He provides for your needs. God could raise your family from the dead if he wanted.

D Yes, it's right to trust God. I love God more than my family.

B So do I.

C I love my family more than God.

X If you were asked to sacrifice your family for God, what would you do?

A (looking at B) Our dad would die for God. So that would be right.

C I wouldn't do it... ever.

D Nor would I.

X OK, if your parents (or carers) were asked by God to sacrifice you, how would you feel?

A OK.

B Yeah… OK.

D Probably OK, but maybe not.

C My dad might do this but he'd be wrong. It wouldn't make me feel great.

EXPERIENCE

The youth leader's (X) experience was to feel shocked by the responses to the story. He found it strange that the teenage boys would generally accept that God might ask for the sacrifice of their lives… literally, and that they would accept this without question. He was a little uncertain at his correctness (as regards the research project) in having asked questions to open up a discussion when it looked as though the young people were not engaging. However, on reflection he felt that he did the right thing in that he presumed their previous familiarity with the story had dulled them as to the terror of the text.

COMMENT

This transcript captures the confusion and angst that has accompanied the reading of this text throughout the centuries. On the one hand there have been those who read the story without terror, linking it to the Jesus story and thinking of his triumphal victory over death, as is alluded to by the writer of the Hebrews when he wrote, "Abraham assumed that if Isaac died, God was able to bring him back again. And, in a sense, Abraham did receive his son back from the dead." (Hebrews 11 v 19).

On the other hand, there are many like Kierkegaard in his seminal book *Fear and Trembling* (1843) who were plagued by the idea of God asking a father to sacrifice a son and who reflected on every angle to achieve a suitable hermeneutic. He was effectively asking if it is possible to make a theological suspension of what is ethical. In other words, whether it is possible to override morality because God has commanded it.

Artists, sculptors and writers have wrestled with the possibility that Isaac offered himself, that Abraham would never have completed his death stroke or that God would never have actually asked for a human sacrifice and that Abraham was merely playing out his cultural expectations as the cult moved from a more primitive form of religion.

This particular conversation shows the interest of teenage boys in the concepts of terror or death and violence. It also shows how familiarity with the sacred text can rob it of its ability to impact when the hearer no longer reflects on its meaning (Pike 2003a). Pike says this can be because the high status of the text can lead to a "too reverential attitude" in the reader.

Prior knowledge of this story had reduced this tale to one that was relatively bland and meaningless. However, the appropriate intervention of the youth leader to apply the story into a more personal context, allowed for reflection to be regained. It is possible to speculate that the literal interpretation offered by some of the boys in affirming the need for human sacrifice if God was to require it, is a fundamentalist interpretation arising from the family home. If this was the case, we would further reflect as to how such a text could be used to justify almost any violence, sacrifice or evil and might be the sort of thinking that could fuel terrorist activity. Alternatively, it could be argued that the youth leader's intervention has not only redeemed the conversation from becoming sterile, but has probed the boys to questioning the interface between their own personal beliefs and their religious tradition.

It is clear that all the boys accepted the text at face value, showing the synthetic-conventional nature of their faith development (Fowler 1981, Stage Three). It can be noted at this stage of tribalizing identity, faith constructs can become ossified if not reflected upon. Alternatively, if the teenager deems that the faith constructs are wrong or irrelevant, they are likely to be disregarded. What is required for a resourceful teenage faith, that will be of value through into adulthood, is the steady re-working and reflection upon the stories of the faith tradition.

Abraham and Isaac (Story 2): Outside the comfort zone
THE CONTEXT
This story was told by a mother (M) to a daughter (D) aged 5.

DISCUSSION

D Why did God ask Abraham to do this horrible thing?

M God was testing Abraham to see it he would trust Him.

D But a friend of God would not kill his son.

M Abraham was a man of great faith.

D I think this could have been sorted out a different way… What is a burnt offering?

M A burnt offering is something you give to God by burning it.

D So Abraham was going to burn his son?

M But he ended up burning a ram.

D Poor ram… But that is better than a boy.

EXPERIENCE

Clearly the mother was concerned at telling such a frightening story to her child and yet felt the need to justify the story. She records, "I approached this session with more than a little trepidation, knowing that the content was likely to be difficult to hear for a young child. I confess that it did make me feel a little uncomfortable the further into the story we got. D's reactions were pretty much as expected. As an adult, I could understand the meaning of the text, but was hesitant about my effectiveness in being able to convey this. Even now, I am unsure as to whether I did it justice. Did I dwell too much on parts of the story? Was I true to the text? Did I endeavour to remove some of the terror? I hope not, as it is a great story of faith and the relationship between God and Abraham is so clearly demonstrated."

COMMENT

The recorded experience of the mother shows considerable self-awareness and a wrestling between her role as a mother and as the one who passes on the story. She is both aware that this story is "outside the comfort zone of a young child's storytime" and that the theological justification for the story is beyond her daughter, yet believes that the story should not be avoided.

This tension is probably what allows this storytelling to be resourceful. Surely the telling of this story in another context, without empathy for the child and with a strong defence of the story's theological justification, would be akin to a form of spiritual abuse.

Abraham and Isaac (Story 3): God's plan "B"

CONTEXT

The story was told by a father (F) to a son aged 7 (A) and a son aged 4 (B).

DISCUSSION AND EXPERIENCE

The following notes were offered by the father, interlacing his experience with the tone of the conversation following an ad-lib account of the story.

F I found this story very uncomfortable to tell – how do you get around the fact that Abraham was expecting to kill Isaac?

B listened carefully to the story without comment. Afterwards he said that he did not like the story because of the naughtiness. (I had not commented on Abraham's morality at that point.) I explained (deviating from the text of course!) that maybe Abraham had misunderstood what God wanted all along – he didn't really want Abraham to kill Isaac. I explained that killing people is wrong, and that I would never hurt him. B however, would not deviate from his opinion. The story was about naughtiness and that was that!

A listened carefully and commented during the story only once, asking why they had gone a long way away. I said I didn't know. I felt a bit more confident about explaining sacrifice to him as a concept, to help him understand what Abraham thought he was doing, although he found this rather odd. I acted out the ram with his curly horns stuck in the bush. Afterwards he asked why God had asked Abraham to act in the way he did. I said I did not know and that I did not understand. I told him I would never hurt him even if I thought God had told me to, but that I didn't think that God would ask that. I said that God probably hadn't meant it because he had provided a plan B – the ram. I also suggested that maybe Abraham had misunderstood God's wishes. This prompted a lot of discussion about plan A and plan B, some of which was rather off the point of the story!

COMMENT

In this instance, where two boys are in the company of a father who is telling the story of Abraham and Isaac, it is entirely appropriate that the father distances himself from the morality shown by Abraham. As a follower of Abraham's God, this father rightly predicts the potential anxiety that could arise from hearing a story that depicts God telling a holy leader to kill his son.

For children at a lower stage of development, it could be very difficult to explain Abraham's actions and so a helpful compromise is offered in terms of Abraham's misunderstanding of God's desire. Putting all the blame for the virtual killing of Isaac upon Abraham's in accurate perception clears God of all blame. This, of course, is academically defensible in that it is likely that Abraham operated in a culture that was responsible for human sacrifice.

Jephthah's Return (Judges 11 v 29–40)

(Judges 11) 29 Then the spirit of the LORD came upon Jephthah, and he passed through Gilead and Manasseh. He passed on to Mizpah of Gilead, and from Mizpah of Gilead he passed on to the Ammonites. 30 And Jephthah made a vow to the LORD, and said, "If you will give the Ammonites into my hand, 31 then whoever comes out of the doors of my house to meet me, when I return victorious from the Ammonites, shall be the Lord's, to be offered up by me as a burnt offering." 32 So Jephthah crossed over to the Ammonites to fight against them; and the LORD gave them into his hand. 33 He inflicted a massive defeat on them from Aroer to the neighborhood of Minnith, twenty towns, and as far as Abel-keramim. So the Ammonites were subdued before the people of Israel. 34 Then Jephthah came to his home at Mizpah; and there was his daughter coming out to meet him with timbrels and with dancing. She was his only child; he had no son or daughter except her. 35 When he saw her, he tore his clothes, and said, "Alas, my daughter! You have brought me very low; you have become the cause of great trouble to me. For I have opened my mouth to the LORD, and I cannot take back my vow." 36 She said to him, "My father, if you have opened your mouth to the LORD, do to me according to what has gone out of your mouth, now that the LORD has given you vengeance against your enemies, the Ammonites." 37 And she said to her father, "Let this thing be done for me: Grant me two months, so that I may go and wander on the mountains, and bewail my virginity, my companions and I." 38 "Go," he said and sent her away for two months. So she departed, she and her companions, and bewailed her virginity on the mountains. 39 At the end of two months, she returned to her father, who did with her according to the vow he had made. She had never slept with a man. So there arose an Israelite custom that 40 for four days every year the daughters of Israel would go out to lament the daughter of Jephthah the Gileadite.

Jephthah's Return (Story 1): The fight wasn't nice

CONTEXT

This story was told by a mother (M) to a son (S) aged 5.

DISCUSSION

S I did not like that story.

M Why was that?

S The fight wasn't nice. (pause) He was not good that that man sent his daughter away.

EXPERIENCE

The mother presumed that her son was bored during the telling of this story, because he sat so quietly and with such a serious face. However, his comments made it clear that he had in fact been listening intently. The young boy's comments appeared profound to the mother because they picked up on her own feelings and understood the pain present in the story.

COMMENT

The child is likely to have mirrored some of the discomfort of the mother as she told a story that was difficult. However, he will not have been able to understand the details of what actually happened, namely that Jephthah was not only sent away by her father, but killed. The horror of the cultural hermeneutic (that grieved Jephthah's death from the male point of view that she had to be killed before she ever slept with a man) is obviously lost on a child but would have been apparent to the mother.

There has been significant debate as to whether it is right to tell stories of pain to a child. Bettelheim (1976) has made a study of the dark meaning in fairy stories and would consider that such stories play a vital part in introducing difficult issues to the growing child. Vygotsky's (1962) work in identifying the place of storytelling at the end of the day to be a "zone of proximal development," perceives that the story of pain, delivered in a known place in the accompanying safety of a secure adult, allows the child to address difficult issues and to begin to process them.

Jephthah's Return (Story 2): Silence
CONTEXT
This story was told by a mother (M) to a daughter (D) aged 7.

DISCUSSION
During the reading of this story, the child, normally engaged, showed no interest and afterwards offered no comment.

After the mother had finished the story and prayed with her (as was their custom) the father stayed with the little girl and asked her if she had enjoyed the story. He received an abrupt "no" in response. In order to leave things on a different note he told his daughter the story reminded him of his trip to Israel with her mother prior to her birth. This engaged her interest and allowed for conversation.

EXPERIENCE
The mother was somewhat perplexed and frustrated by this lack of response to a difficult story and presumed that it had not been understood. However the one comment that did materialize was that Jephthah had only one daughter, just like she was the only daughter in this family.

The mother's reflection was that she should return to this genre at a later stage, select a different story and see if this produced a response.

COMMENT

This text of terror has very likely lived up to its name. The child has listened and internalized her responses, offering a surface disinterest and lack of engagement. Her one comment shows her identification with the daughter of Jephthah. She also recalled the story at a later point when listening to the story of Noah. On that occasion she confused Noah's son Japheth with Jephthah. In order to cope with the story she has most probably tried to deflect it.

In this situation, the parents did well to remain aware of the possible emotions by moving attention onto a more secure theme – namely the history of their marriage. However, the story is calling for more response when told to a young child and may well require some parental comment that distances itself from the brutal and archaic actions of Jephthah. There are some stories that a Christian parent cannot defend to their child as being appropriate and this must surely be one of them. This lack of comment or silence might be interpreted as acquiescence to the killing of a daughter by a parent fulfilling the requirements of a just God.

Jepthah's Return (Story 3): Think before you speak

CONTEXT

This story was told by a mother (M) to a son aged 10 (S) and a daughter aged 8 (D).

DISCUSSION

D I didn't get that! (pause) Why would he do that though? I thought God didn't like sacrifices. Did he kill her as soon as he walked in? Wouldn't he forget about it after two months?

M He had made a promise to God.

S Why make a promise like that? He didn't have to say he'd kill someone like that – he could have offered crops or something.

D Yeah... (pause).
Did God accept it? I don't think he should! (pause).
I suppose he had to keep his word but if it was your best mate, you'd
feel really nervous about asking God if you could change your mind...
(pause).
No, I think it's wrong. The message is, "Think before you say!" I think
he shouldn't have killed her like that!

S How can you like God if you're going to be sacrificed?

D Only a member of your family would be in the house. Maybe one of
his family was annoying him and he wanted to kill them... But he
didn't stop and think it would be his daughter who might come out.
I don't think he should have made that promise.

S I wouldn't sacrifice for any reason! Why don't you give God something special... but not a human being, not your own daughter... like
one of his animals or a special item of clothing. He really should have
thought through what he was saying.

D The moral is, "Think before you speak". He should have asked God to
let him off. He could have said sorry and he'd do something else for
God to replace the sacrifice and something else to say sorry.

EXPERIENCE

The mother records being surprised by these comments and by the energy
of the response. She was interested to see her children endeavouring to
work out for themselves the purpose of sacrifice, having not looked at
such a story before. She was very aware that they were struggling to make
sense of the story and to find a meaningful purpose.

COMMENT

There is considerable feeling in this interchange in which the younger child (the daughter) is the first to speak, which is in itself unusual. She maintains her flow of thought for quite a while. There is no mistaking that she is appalled by Jephthah's actions. Her brother then joins in and mirrors her comments, empowering her contribution. It ends by the daughter once more repeating that Jephthah has got it wrong. She has the last word.

It is interesting to note the harmony of a brother and sister, united in defying what they rightly consider to be a shocking story of human sacrifice. What stands out as being unusual is the mother's surprise at the children's response. Although she appears to be an empathetic mother, as she is aware that this is a "text of terror", she has not recognized the effect of such a story on her children. The shock upon them is the double effect of their close identification with the child-object of sacrifice and the fact that this action is of current potential danger to them in that the story is about a God who is worshipped in the family home and Church.

Maybe this is the heart of the problem – both the mother and the children have accepted that this God is one that needs appeasing, one that will not change his mind and worse still, somehow connected to the God of their faith. It is the young boy who sums up the children's anxiety, "How can you like God if you're going to be sacrificed?"

Jephthah's Return (Story 4): A promise is a promise
CONTEXT
This story was told by a mother (M) to a daughter (D) aged 10.

DISCUSSION

D What on earth was all that about? I did understand it, even though there were a lot of long words, I just didn't get why that man had to kill his daughter.

M He had made a promise to God to give him the first person he saw on his return home.

D Well in that case a promise is a promise. It serves him right if he made a promise he couldn't keep.

M So what do you think about it?

D It's not a long story and it's quite violent.

EXPERIENCE

The mother found the reading of this passage fairly difficult due to the unusual names as well as the content. As a result, after the event she looked this unfamiliar story up in her own Bible to consider the context in which it was set.

COMMENT

It is interesting to notice that this girl did not particularly empathize with Jephthah's daughter and showed no moral outrage nor fear in Jephthah's actions. Her concern was more to do with the correctness of keeping one's word when a promise has been made.

However, there is a sense that she does not believe that a father will kill his daughter when she says, "It serves him right if he made a promise he couldn't keep."

Ananias and Sapphira (Acts 5 v 1–11)

(Acts 5) But a man named Ananias, with the consent of his wife Sapphira, sold a piece of property; 2 with his wife's knowledge, he kept back some of the proceeds, and brought only a part and laid it at the apostles' feet. 3 "Ananias," Peter asked, "why has Satan filled your heart to lie to the Holy Spirit and to keep back part of the proceeds of the land? 4 While it remained unsold, did it not remain your own? And after it was sold, were not the proceeds at your disposal? How is it that you have contrived this deed in your heart? You did not lie to us but to God!" 5 Now when Ananias heard these words, he fell down and died. And great fear seized all who heard of it. 6 The young men came and wrapped up his body, then carried him out and buried him. 7 After an interval of about three hours his wife came in, not knowing what had happened. 8 Peter said to her, "Tell me whether you and your husband sold the land for such and such a price." And she said, "Yes, that was the price." 9 Then Peter said to her, "How is it that you have agreed together to put the Spirit of the Lord to the test? Look, the feet of those who have buried your husband are at the door, and they will carry you out." 10 Immediately she fell down at his feet and died. When the young men came in they found her dead, so they carried her out and buried her beside her husband. 11 And great fear seized the whole church and all who heard of these things.

Ananias and Saphira (Story 1): A Nazi propaganda story

CONTEXT

This story was told by a father (F) to two teenage sons aged 17 (A) and 14 (B).

DISCUSSION

This story was initially set in context by F who said that in the first days of the early church, believers expected Jesus to return any day and so were less worried about finance and the future, sometimes giving up their jobs. In this instance he said that they were encouraged to sell up their homes, pool their resources and live in a sort of community. After the telling of this story, B was quick to comment.

B Flipping eck! That's Nazi!

A Yes, it's a propaganda story. The apostles equate the Holy Spirit with themselves and made the presumption that they know exactly what is right. They are in fact manipulating and deceiving Saphira. Look, they didn't even tell her that her husband is dead and proceed to trap her.

B This story would make the community of the early church well scared! It would be a way of threatening them to behave in the way the apostles want.

A (After pause). But I think we need to be liberal in how we understand this story. It is demonstrating literally that, "The wages of sin is death", but it is likely to be an exaggerated propaganda story, manipulating people into doing good... (pause)... If the Holy Spirit was actually involved, he'd win you into good ways, not threaten you by fear.

F So you cope with this by seeing it as an exaggerated story?

A Yes. It is retro. The early church is thinking of an Old Testament God... you know a judgemental one. They are hankering after an earlier understanding. If they believed like this, everyone would get killed by the Holy Spirit.

B Maybe the story's about eternal life. These deaths were not so bad (as they went to heaven) but it's more of a warning.

A It's nonetheless challenging and without much forgiveness. But yes, it reminds us that Jesus is into tough stuff too.

EXPERIENCE

The father was intrigued by the level of feeling aroused by this story. The outburst from his sons was sustained for some time, despite the fact that they were tired. He wondered how much influence was had by other conversations about the Nazi war machine.

COMMENT

Despite the need to distance themselves from the theology of this story, there was a strong attempt by the boys to reconcile themselves with it as well. They came up with two possible solutions; one that the story was exaggerated by the early church and the other that it was part of a developmental phase as the early church moved from law to grace. The final comment that suggests a tension in the gospel and in the person of Jesus allows for considerable room for manoeuvre in handling this story and in handling faith as they develop.

Chapter 4

Texts of Justice and Judgement

Banishment from Eden (Genesis 3)

(Genesis 3) Now the serpent was more crafty than any other wild animal that the LORD God had made. He said to the woman, "Did God say, "You shall not eat from any tree in the garden"?" 2 The woman said to the serpent, "We may eat of the fruit of the trees in the garden; 3 but God said, 'You shall not eat of the fruit of the tree that is in the middle of the garden, nor shall you touch it, or you shall die.'" 4 But the serpent said to the woman, "You will not die; 5 for God knows that when you eat of it your eyes will be opened, and you will be like God, knowing good and evil." 6 So when the woman saw that the tree was good for food, and that it was a delight to the eyes, and that the tree was to be desired to make one wise, she took of its fruit and ate; and she also gave some to her husband, who was with her, and he ate. 7 Then the eyes of both were opened, and they knew that they were naked; and they sewed fig leaves together and made loincloths for themselves. 8 They heard the sound of the LORD God walking in the garden at the time of the evening breeze, and the man and his wife hid themselves from the presence of the LORD God among the trees of the garden. 9 But the LORD God called to the man, and said to him, "Where are you?" 10 He said, "I heard the sound of you in the garden, and I was afraid, because I was naked; and I hid myself." 11 He said, "Who told you that you were naked? Have you eaten from the tree of which I commanded you not to eat?" 12 The man said, "The woman whom you gave to be with me, she gave me fruit from the tree, and I ate." 13 Then the LORD God said to the woman, "What is this that you have done?" The woman said, "The serpent tricked me, and I ate." 14 The LORD God said to the serpent, "Because you have done this, cursed are you among all animals and among all wild creatures; upon your belly you shall go, and dust you shall eat all the days of your life. 15 I will put enmity between you and the woman, and between your offspring and hers; he will strike your head, and you will strike his heel." 16 To the woman he said, "I will greatly increase your pangs in childbearing; in pain you shall bring forth children, yet your desire shall be for your husband, and he shall rule over you." 17 And to the man he said, "Because you have listened to the voice of your wife, and have eaten of the tree about which I commanded you, 'You shall not eat of it,' cursed is the ground because of you; in toil you shall eat of it all the days of your life; 18 thorns and thistles it shall bring forth for you; and you shall eat the plants of the field. 19 By the sweat of your face you shall eat bread until you return to the ground, for out of it you were taken; you are dust, and to dust you shall return." 20 The man named his wife Eve, because she was the mother of all living. 21 And the LORD God made garments of skins for the man and for his wife, and clothed them. 22 Then the LORD God said, "See, the man has become like one of us, knowing good and evil; and now, he might reach out his hand and take also from the tree of life, and eat, and live forever" – 23 therefore the LORD God sent him forth from the

garden of Eden, to till the ground from which he was taken. 24
He drove out the man; and at the east of the garden of Eden he
placed the cherubim, and a sword flaming and turning to guard
the way to the tree of life.

Banishment from Eden (Story 1): The serpent that was tricked by the devil
CONTEXT

This story was told by a mother (M) to a son aged 10 (S) and a daughter
aged 8 (D).

DISCUSSION

M Well, what do you think of this story?

D I thought Christians weren't meant to believe in curses!

S No, but the story's about Adam and Eve and God telling them not to
   eat it and the snake told the woman to, and she told Adam. Then God
   found out and *then* he cursed them. (Checking text)... He cursed the
   ground and the serpent.

D He did it by making Eve have pain when she had children and making
   Adam eat bread and plants for the rest of his life.

S Yeah, but isn't God meant to be forgiving?

D But this is from the Old Testament – Jesus hasn't been killed yet, so he
   didn't know about that yet.

S The serpent should get punished most, Eve a bit less and Adam less,
   because he only did what Eve told him. (Pause)
   By the way, why would you have a tree in your garden you can't eat
   from? Why wouldn't you get rid of it and plant another one?

D And why would the serpent want to trick them anyway? What if the
   devil made the serpent do that?

S They hid from God because they didn't want him to know. God wouldn't want Adam and Eve to eat it because he didn't want them to be like him.

D But God wouldn't do that because he loves us; maybe he was trying to give them a test to see if they were trustworthy. They didn't pass the test.

(Reflectively) You know there's different ways of stories being told, like legends and stuff – so what if Adam wasn't there with Eve, so he didn't know it was fruit from *that* tree. It wouldn't be his fault then.

M No. Then it would be a different story.

EXPERIENCE

The mother enjoyed this session and was fascinated at how the children worked independently of her in trying to question and understand the story and find explanations for some of the actions in it. She felt they were relaxed and had an overriding assumption that God loves us and was not acting in a malevolent way. This gave them freedom to question.

COMMENT

This recorded dialogue is of huge value, coming from the hidden place of a secure home where key stage two children (aged 7–11) are able to question each other in the safe environment of a parent.

Their contributions are initially gender specific, with the boy pointing out that Adam deserved least punishment and the girl noticing the resultant pains of childbirth.

Some fascinating questions are posed as the story is reflected upon. The boy wants to know where forgiveness lies and the girl suggests that because it occurs prior to the Christ event, that God had not discovered forgiveness (a truly radical idea to a conventional believer).

Other questions remain unanswered, with reflections being offered about a tree that was entirely aesthetic, about this serpent being tricked by the devil, about God being insecure in his identity (not wanting his creation to be like him) and by the whole event being prompted by ignorance and not by disobedience.

These reflections would not go amiss in an adult theological discussion concerning the origins of sin or the creation of evil. Indeed, they offer something of the original vision of a child.

Incidentally, in talking with adults, I am often intrigued to notice that the serpent in this story is presumed to be one and the same as the devil, an insight of which these children are happily unaware. The text does not suggest the dualistic idea that the devil is present at the birth of creation; rather it is an idea that has emerged from Augustine and popularized at a later stage by Calvin.

Obviously there is another sense in which this conversation depicts a child's evolving comprehension in that the story is always taken at a literal level and not reflected upon as being metaphorical or allegorical.

Banishment from Eden (Story 2): An odd story of people wearing leaves
CONTEXT
This story was told by a father (F) to a son aged 7 (A) and a son aged 4 (B).

DISCUSSION AND EXPERIENCE
I had assumed that both boys knew the story. B recognized the names Adam and Eve immediately, and wanted to show me his Adam and Eve jigsaw straight away (even though I'd seen it on many occasions before)! However, he could only tell me that they "lived in a zoo". A knew that they lived in the Garden of Eden, but was still much less familiar with the story than I had expected.

A commented that a walking, talking snake was similar to a character in a favourite children's cartoon series "Go Diego." Both boys were very interested in the clothes. A commented that it would be difficult to wear leaves if they were still on branches, and we enjoyed thinking up silly ways you could wear leaves that were still on trees. I explained to B that God made clothes out of animal skins that the animals didn't want any more, and he said that was like making things out of discarded reindeer antlers.

B said he did not like the story because of the "bad behaviour". A, who is mildly autistic, could not answer when asked directly what he thought, but agreed out of a choice of "odd" or "enjoyable" he would choose "odd".

COMMENT

It is interesting to hear the Garden of Eden described as a zoo, but this is probably a dominant image in the mind of many children.

So too is the idea of wearing leaves – an idea that is interesting and comical. To engage with a young mind with such fresh imagery is to find a new way into a well-known story – even if the actual meaning is barely touched upon.

Noah's Ark (Genesis 6–9 v 19)

(Genesis 6) When people began to multiply on the face of the ground, and daughters were born to them, 2 the sons of God saw that they were fair; and they took wives for themselves of all that they chose. 3 Then the LORD said, "My spirit shall not abide in mortals forever, for they are flesh; their days shall be one hundred twenty years." 4 The Nephilim were on the earth in those days – and also afterward – when the sons of God went in to the daughters of humans, who bore children to them. These were the heroes that were of old, warriors of renown. 5 The LORD saw that the wickedness of humankind was great in the earth, and that every inclination of the thoughts of their hearts was only evil continually. 6 And the LORD was sorry that he had made humankind on the earth, and it grieved him to his heart. 7 So the LORD said, "I will blot out from the earth the human beings I have created – people together with animals and creeping things and birds of the air, for I am sorry that I have made them." 8 But Noah found favour in the sight of the LORD. 9 These are the descendants of Noah. Noah was a righteous man, blameless in his generation; Noah walked with God. 10 And Noah had three sons, Shem, Ham, and Japheth. 11 Now the earth was corrupt in God's sight, and the earth was filled with violence. 12 And God saw that the earth was corrupt; for all flesh had corrupted its ways upon the earth. 13 And God said to Noah, "I have determined to make an end of all flesh, for the earth is filled with violence because of them; now I am going to destroy them along with the earth. 14 Make yourself an ark of cypress wood; make rooms in the ark, and cover it inside and out with pitch. 15 This is how you are to make it: the length of the ark three hundred cubits, its width fifty cubits, and its height thirty cubits. 16 Make a roof for the ark, and finish it to a cubit above; and put the door of the ark in its side; make it with lower, second, and third decks. 17 For my part, I am going to bring a flood of waters on the earth, to destroy from under heaven all flesh in which is the breath of life; everything that is on the earth shall die. 18 But I will establish my covenant with you; and you shall come into the ark, you, your sons, your wife, and your sons' wives with you. 19 And of every living thing, of all flesh, you shall bring two of every kind into the ark, to keep them alive with you; they shall be male and female. 20 Of the birds according to their kinds, and of the animals according to their kinds, of every creeping thing of the ground according to its kind, two of every kind shall come in to you, to keep them alive. 21 Also take with you every kind of food that is eaten, and store it up; and it shall serve as food for you and for them." 22 Noah did this; he did all that God commanded him.

(Genesis 7) Then the LORD said to Noah, "Go into the ark, you and all your household, for I have seen that you alone are righteous before me in this generation. 2 Take with you seven pairs of all clean animals, the male and its mate; and a pair of the animals that are not clean, the male and its mate; 3 and seven pairs of the birds of the air also, male and female, to keep their kind alive on the face of all the earth. 4 For in seven days I will send rain on the earth for forty days and forty nights; and every living thing that I have made I will blot out from the face of the ground." 5 And Noah did all that the LORD had commanded him. 6 Noah was six hundred years old when the flood of waters came on the earth. 7 And Noah with his sons and his wife and his sons' wives went into the ark to escape the waters of the flood. 8 Of clean animals, and of animals that are not clean, and of birds, and of everything that creeps on the ground, 9 two and two, male and female, went into the ark with Noah, as God had commanded Noah. 10 And after seven days the waters of the flood came on the earth. 11 In the six hundredth year of Noah's life, in the second month, on the seventeenth day of the month, on that day all the fountains of the great deep burst forth, and the windows of the heavens were opened. 12 The rain fell on the earth forty days and forty nights. 13 On the very same day Noah with his sons, Shem and Ham and Japheth, and Noah's wife and the three wives of his sons entered the ark, 14 they and every wild animal of every kind, and all domestic animals of every kind, and every creeping thing that creeps on the earth, and every bird of every kind – every bird, every winged creature. 15 They went into the ark with Noah, two and two of all flesh in which there was the breath of life. 16 And those that entered, male and female of all flesh, went in as God had commanded him; and the LORD shut him in. 17 The flood continued forty days on the earth; and the waters increased, and bore up the ark, and it rose high above the earth. 18 The waters swelled and increased greatly on the earth; and the ark floated on the face of the waters. 19 The waters swelled so mightily on the earth that all the high mountains under the whole heaven were covered; 20 the waters swelled above the mountains, covering them fifteen cubits deep. 21 And all flesh died that moved on the earth, birds, domestic animals, wild animals, all swarming creatures that swarm on the earth, and all human beings; 22 everything on dry land in whose nostrils was the breath of life died. 23 He blotted out every living thing that was on the face of the ground, human beings and animals and creeping things and birds of the air; they were blotted out from the earth. Only Noah was left, and those that were with him in the ark. 24 And the waters swelled on the earth for one hundred fifty days.

(Genesis 8) But God remembered Noah and all the wild animals and all the domestic animals that were with him in the ark. And God made a wind blow over the earth, and the waters subsided; 2 the fountains of the deep and the windows of the heavens were closed, the rain from the heavens was restrained, 3 and the waters gradually receded from the earth. At the end of one hundred fifty days the waters had abated; 4 and in the seventh month, on the seventeenth day of the month, the ark came to rest on the mountains of Ararat. 5 The waters continued to abate until the tenth month; in the tenth month, on the first day of the month, the tops of the mountains appeared. 6 At the end of forty days Noah opened the window of the ark that he had made 7 and sent out the raven; and it went to and fro until the waters were dried up from the earth. 8 Then he sent out the dove from him, to see if the waters had subsided from the face of the ground; 9 but the dove found no place to set its foot, and it returned to him to the ark, for the waters were still on the face of the whole earth. So he put out his hand and took it and brought it into the ark with him. 10 He waited another seven days, and again he sent out the dove from the ark; 11 and the dove came back to him in the evening, and there in its beak was a freshly plucked olive leaf; so Noah knew that the waters had subsided from the earth. 12 Then he waited another seven days, and sent out the dove; and it did not return to him any more. 13 In the six hundred first year, in the first month, the first day of the month, the waters were dried up from the earth; and Noah removed the covering of the ark, and looked, and saw that the face of the ground was drying. 14 In the second month, on the twenty-seventh day of the month, the earth was dry. 15 Then God said to Noah, 16 "Go out of the ark, you and your wife, and your sons and your sons' wives with you. 17 Bring out with you every living thing that is with you of all flesh – birds and animals and every creeping thing that creeps on the earth – so that they may abound on the earth, and be fruitful and multiply on the earth." 18 So Noah went out with his sons and his wife and his sons' wives. 19 And every animal, every creeping thing, and every bird, everything that moves on the earth, went out of the ark by families. 20 Then Noah built an altar to the LORD, and took of every clean animal and of every clean bird, and offered burnt offerings on the altar. 21 And when the LORD smelled the pleasing odour, the LORD said in his heart, "I will never again curse the ground because of humankind, for the inclination of the human heart is evil from youth; nor will I ever again destroy every living creature as I have done. 22 As long as the earth endures, seedtime and harvest, cold and heat, summer and winter, day and night, shall not cease."

(Genesis 9) God blessed Noah and his sons, and said to them, "Be fruitful and multiply, and fill the earth. 2 The fear and dread of you shall rest on every animal of the earth, and on every bird of the air, on everything that creeps on the ground, and on all the fish of the sea; into your hand they are delivered. 3 Every moving thing that lives shall be food for you; and just as I gave you the green plants, I give you everything. 4 Only, you shall not eat flesh with its life, that is, its blood. 5 For your own lifeblood I will surely require a reckoning: from every animal I will require it and from human beings, each one for the blood of another, I will require a reckoning for human life. 6 Whoever sheds the blood of a human, by a human shall that person's blood be shed; for in his own image God made humankind. 7 And you, be fruitful and multiply, abound on the earth and multiply in it." 8 Then God said to Noah and to his sons with him, 9 "As for me, I am establishing my covenant with you and your descendants after you, 10 and with every living creature that is with you, the birds, the domestic animals, and every animal of the earth with you, as many as came out of the ark. 11 I establish my covenant with you, that never again shall all flesh be cut off by the waters of a flood, and never again shall there be a flood to destroy the earth." 12 God said, "This is the sign of the covenant that I make between me and you and every living creature that is with you, for all future generations: 13 I have set my bow in the clouds, and it shall be a sign of the covenant between me and the earth. 14 When I bring clouds over the earth and the bow is seen in the clouds, 15 I will remember my covenant that is between me and you and every living creature of all flesh; and the waters shall never again become a flood to destroy all flesh. 16 When the bow is in the clouds, I will see it and remember the everlasting covenant between God and every living creature of all flesh that is on the earth." 17 God said to Noah, "This is the sign of the covenant that I have established between me and all flesh that is on the earth." 18 The sons of Noah who went out of the ark were Shem, Ham, and Japheth. Ham was the father of Canaan. 19 These three were the sons of Noah; and from these the whole earth was peopled.

Noah's Ark (Story 1): Eighty-year-old Noah

CONTEXT

This story was told by a mother (M) to a daughter (D) aged 7.

DISCUSSION

This story was well-known to the child who at the age of four (three years previously) had been involved with her family overseas in a children's workshop that had considered the story of Noah's Ark in four languages.

D This story is a bit longer than other books telling the stories. It repeats stuff.

M Yes, it does.

D It also goes on for ages about how long the ark is to be and how high. (All this was not present in the other children's paraphrases known to her.)
Did you say that Noah was 600 years old?

M Yes.

D Do you think he was really that old?

M I think his age was stated to show that he was a very wise man who had authority.

D Ah! He was probably about eighty then.

M Maybe.

D So one of Noah's sons was that silly man who sent his daughter away (she was thinking of Jephthah and confusing him with Noah's son, called Japheth).

M Maybe.

EXPERIENCE

On reflection, the mother records that she was feeling tired and because the text was so long, she did not have the energy to have a discussion about the different sources in this story, nor the issues of historical accuracy. However, she agreed that the time was right to tell a full length script of a story her daughter had heard many times. She was surprised at her daughter's recall of the name Jephthah in confusing it with Japheth, an error she did not correct at the time.

COMMENT

This conversation shows the child reworking a story that was familiar. This is what happens to all stories that are re-told over life, each telling bringing different meaning, understanding and connections. Whereas for the adult, much of this involves the reworking of memories and association, for a child it is more likely to do with the development of cognition.

In this instance, it is interesting to note the child learning to de-code her mother's comment concerning Noah's age. The daughter questioned the huge age of Noah (600 years) as being literally accurate and the mother offered a metaphorical interpretation which the daughter went on to specify as meaning "about eighty years old." This shows the child grappling with issues of literalism and symbolism and learning to interpret what her mother thinks as well as what she thinks herself.

Noah's Ark (Story 2): Who built the ark?

CONTEXT

This story was told by a mother (M) to a daughter (D) aged 5.

DISCUSSION

Although this story was familiar to the child, she found the language of the original text quite challenging.

She liked the fact that Noah was given such good instructions about how to build the ark and that a large number of animals were to be saved. She enjoyed the account of the dove being sent out.

Before tiredness took over, the mother initiated a brief discussion as to why God became so angry with people that he caused a flood and why Noah was so special as to be the one who was saved along with his family. After this, the child began to sing a song that she knew called, "Who built the ark?"

EXPERIENCE

The mother was torn between remaining at the surface level of the story and taking the conversation down into the realm of deeper meaning. As a teacher she knew that a five-year-old would only be able to go a certain distance, but as a mother she felt her child might go further.

COMMENT

The story of Noah's Ark is often told to children in order to highlight the role of animals, a boat in a rainstorm and a rainbow. The religious meaning is therefore something to do with God's creativity and his on-going faithfulness in creation.

The story however, is far more complex and is about judgement of sin on all creation demonstrated in a widespread flood. The religious meaning is actually about God's justice that metes out judgement whilst also offering salvation.

This process of how the text of the story of Noah's Ark is edited has been noted in wider research (Worsley 2004) where it is illustrated that a Moslem child candidly referred to the horror of the story's judgement narrative in stark contrast to other Christian children who offer versions of a more comforting and colourful drama. This research presumes that these differences are due to the different cultural backgrounds in which the stories are told. The Islamic hermeneutic is frank about the story's actual meaning to be about judgement whereas the Christian hermeneutic is less comfortable with this harsh message being told to children.

As a result, the layering of meaning in this story makes it an ideal narrative to be re-told as a child matures. If the story remains at a simplistic Sunday school level, it will be relegated to the realm of naive fantasy by the growing child. If it is discussed, the story can be increasingly understood to belong to a genre of historical myth that contains important theological reflection.

Noah's Ark (Story 3): Is the flood like a tsunami?

CONTEXT

This story was told by a father (F) to a son aged 10 (S) and a daughter aged 8 (D).

DISCUSSION

D Wouldn't Noah have had lots of notes about all the things he had to do and collect? Not only the animals but everything they eat?

S And some animals might eat the others. For example, lions eat antelope.

D Surely they'd have lots of insects?

S What about the fish?

F But God had to cause a flood because the world was full of sin and it was too much to ask to have God just sit there relaxed, doing nothing.

S Are the floods in Africa or Asia the same thing? Or the tsunami?

F They are big floods for a period of time, but we don't know that they are sent by God like this one.

S (Commenting on 9: 19) Wow, I'm related to Noah. Did the people have any warning of what was going to happen if they didn't stop sinning?

D Where did all the water go?

S 'Cos Noah did everything God asked before the ark and after it, he allowed him to live for over 600 years.

D God spoke to Noah several times. Why doesn't he speak to us like that any more?

S How did he know which was a good specimen of animals?

D I think the story is true. God can do practically anything.

EXPERIENCE

The father was amused and surprised by this conversation, particularly their logic about animals, insects, fish and note-taking. He felt that it was because the children knew the story so well, they had developed some strong questions which they were comfortable leaving unanswered. He was glad to notice this lack of anxiety in the face of uncertainty. He further noted that a lot of their questions echoed the sort of questions adults ask about this story.

COMMENT

This conversation offers flashes of complexity and simplicity, moving from the childish to the sophisticated and then away again. It is this movement from one thing to another that signals that it is a conversation between children.

At one point they are interested in the logistics of fitting all creatures into the ark and then they are asking whether the judgement of the flood is occurring at this point in history. Then, before the power of this question is allowed to settle, connections are made with the bloodline of Noah. The notion of forgiveness of sin and the prevention of the flood briefly appears before other logical questions occur concerning the location of flood waters, how God speaks and the choice of animals for survival. All these questions are then deftly put away with the statement, "God can do practically anything."

In this sentence, it is amusing to hear the word "practically". The children are comfortable in their sense of a big and righteous God, but their spirit of reflective questioning has cautioned them not to be too definite. Therefore rather than saying God can do anything, they say he can do practically anything.

This conversation is a good example of how children learn by testing the boundaries in a safe place. Rather than being met with a credal certainty or by closed answers, they are allowed to play with concepts. They have not as yet queried whether the story is mythical but within a literalist worldview, they feel that everything is up for testing. This will pave the way for their faith to be contextualized and owned in the future, though it does ensure their credal orthodoxy.

The Sheep and the Goats (Matthew 25 v 31–46)

(Matthew 25) 31 "When the Son of Man comes in his glory, and all the angels with him, then he will sit on the throne of his glory. 32 All the nations will be gathered before him, and he will separate people one from another as a shepherd separates the sheep from the goats, 33 and he will put the sheep at his right hand and the goats at the left. 34 Then the king will say to those at his right hand, "Come, you that are blessed by my Father, inherit the kingdom prepared for you from the foundation of the world; 35 for I was hungry and you gave me food, I was thirsty and you gave me something to drink, I was a stranger and you welcomed me, 36 I was naked and you gave me clothing, I was sick and you took care of me, I was in prison and you visited me." 37 Then the righteous will answer him, "Lord, when was it that we saw you hungry and gave you food, or thirsty and gave you something to drink? 38 And when was it that we saw you a stranger and welcomed you, or naked and gave you clothing? 39 And when was it that we saw you sick or in prison and visited you?" 40 And the king will answer them, "Truly I tell you, just as you did it to one of the least of these who are members of my family, you did it to me." 41 Then he will say to those at his left hand, "You that are accursed, depart from me into the eternal fire prepared for the devil and his angels; 42 for I was hungry and you gave me no food, I was thirsty and you gave me nothing to drink, 43 I was a stranger and you did not welcome me, naked and you did not give me clothing, sick and in prison and you did not visit me." 44 Then they also will answer, "Lord, when was it that we saw you hungry or thirsty or a stranger or naked or sick or in prison, and did not take care of you?" 45 Then he will answer them, "Truly I tell you, just as you did not do it to one of the least of these, you did not do it to me." 46 And these will go away into eternal punishment, but the righteous into eternal life."

The Sheep and the Goats (Story 1): Good people get bread

CONTEXT

This story was told by a mother (M) to a son (S) aged 5.

DISCUSSION

As the story was read, the young boy listened carefully and laughed every time the word "naked" was mentioned (v 37, 38, 43 and 44).

S That was quite a good story.

M What did you like about it?

S I liked the story being about sick people and people in prison who obey God. He helps them.

M How does God help them?

S If the people are good they get bread and if they are very, very good they get a drink.

EXPERIENCE

The mother found her son's interest in the word "naked" amusing and was initially concerned that his comprehension was not quite accurate. On reflection she thought his understanding was not a problem in that he had related the story to obeying God and helping people who are in difficulties.

COMMENT

The gist of the story is clear to the five-year-old but the details of judgement and the metaphors of sheep and goats are not.

It is possible that the child's response to God's favour being seen in bread and drink is a reflection on how the child understands Holy Communion. The notion "If the people are good they get bread and if they are very, very good they get a drink" is the sort of literalist connection to the sacraments that might be made by a five-year-old immersed in a religious tradition.

The Sheep and the Goats (Story 2): That'll teach you to be naughty
CONTEXT
This story was told by a mother (M) to a daughter (D) aged 10.

DISCUSSION

D Well, that'll teach you to be naughty.

M What do you mean?

D Well, the good people get to go to heaven and the bad people don't.

M And are you one of the good or the bad people?

D I'm a mixture of both sheep and goat.

M What is the goat bit in you?

D It is hard being nice to people I don't like.

M What sort of people are those?

D People who don't like me. It is hard to be nice to people all the time.

M Have you any other comments about the story?

D No, that's enough.

EXPERIENCE

The mother found this to be a fairly straightforward storytelling session.

COMMENT

The young girl's moral absolutes are softened by her realization that she is a mixture of sheep and goats. A development of this concept will probably allow her to be more forgiving of those who are naughty, or the naughty bit inside everyone.

Chapter 5

Texts of Comfort
and Hope

David and Goliath (1 Samuel 17 v 1–54)

(1 Samuel 17) Now the Philistines gathered their armies for battle; they were gathered at Socoh, which belongs to Judah, and encamped between Socoh and Azekah, in Ephes-dammim. 2 Saul and the Israelites gathered and encamped in the valley of Elah, and formed ranks against the Philistines. 3 The Philistines stood on the mountain on the one side, and Israel stood on the mountain on the other side, with a valley between them. 4 And there came

out from the camp of the Philistines a champion named Goliath, of Gath, whose height was six cubits and a span. 5 He had a helmet of bronze on his head, and he was armed with a coat of mail; the weight of the coat was five thousand shekels of bronze. 6 He had greaves of bronze on his legs and a javelin of bronze slung between his shoulders. 7 The shaft of his spear was like a weaver's beam, and his spear's head weighed six hundred shekels of iron; and his shield-bearer went before him. 8 He stood and shouted to the ranks of Israel, "Why have you come out to draw up for battle? Am I not a Philistine, and are you not servants of Saul? Choose a man for yourselves, and let him come down to me. 9 If he is able to fight with me and kill me, then we will be your servants; but if I prevail against him and kill him, then you shall be our servants and serve us." 10 And the Philistine said, "Today I defy the ranks of Israel! Give me a man, that we may fight together." 11 When Saul and all Israel heard these words of the Philistine, they were dismayed and greatly afraid. 12 Now David was the son of an Ephrathite of Bethlehem in Judah, named Jesse, who had eight sons. In the days of Saul the man was already old and advanced in years. 13 The three eldest sons of Jesse had followed Saul to the battle; the names of his three sons who went to the battle were Eliab the firstborn, and next to him Abinadab, and the third Shammah. 14 David was the youngest; the three eldest followed Saul, 15 but David went back and forth from Saul to feed his father's sheep at Bethlehem. 16 For forty days the Philistine came forward and took his stand, morning and evening. 17 Jesse said to his son David, "Take for your brothers an ephah of this parched grain and these ten loaves, and carry them quickly to the camp to your brothers; 18 also take these ten cheeses to the commander of their thousand. See how your brothers fare, and bring some token from them." 19 Now Saul, and they, and all the men of Israel, were in the valley of Elah, fighting with the Philistines. 20 David rose early in the morning, left the sheep with a keeper, took the provisions, and went as Jesse had commanded him. He came to the encampment as the army was going forth to the battle line, shouting the war cry. 21 Israel and the Philistines drew up for battle, army against army. 22 David left the things in charge of the keeper of the baggage, ran to the ranks, and went and greeted his brothers. 23 As he talked with them, the champion, the Philistine of Gath, Goliath by name, came up out of the ranks of the Philistines, and spoke the same words as before. And David heard him. 24 All the Israelites, when they saw the man, fled from him and were very much afraid. 25 The Israelites said, "Have you seen this man who has come up? Surely he has come up to defy Israel. The king will greatly enrich the man who kills him, and will give him his daughter and make his family free in Israel." 26 David said to the men who stood by him, "What shall be done for the man who kills this Philistine, and takes away the reproach from Israel? For who is this uncircumcised Philistine that he should defy the armies of the living God?" 27 The people answered him in the same way, "So shall it be done for the man who kills him." 28 His eldest brother Eliab heard him talking to the men; and Eliab's anger was kindled against David. He said, "Why have you come down? With whom have you left those few sheep in the wilderness? I know your presumption and the evil of your heart; for you have come down just to see the battle." 29 David said, "What have I done now? It was only a question." 30 He turned away from him toward another and spoke in the same way; and the people answered him again as before. 31 When the words that David spoke were heard, they repeated them before Saul; and he sent for him. 32 David said to Saul, "Let no one's heart fail because of him; your servant will go and fight with this Philistine." 33 Saul said to David, "You are not able to go against this Philistine to fight with him; for you are just a boy, and he has been a warrior from his youth." 34 But David said to Saul, "Your servant used to keep sheep for his father; and whenever a lion or a bear came, and took a lamb from the flock, 35 I went after it and struck it down, rescuing the lamb from its mouth; and if it turned against me, I would catch it by the jaw, strike it down, and kill it. 36 Your servant has killed both lions and bears; and this uncircumcised Philistine shall be like one of them, since he has defied the armies of the living God." 37 David said, "The LORD, who saved me from the paw of the lion and from the paw of the bear, will save me from the hand of this Philistine." So Saul said to David, "Go, and may the LORD be with you!" 38 Saul clothed David with his armour; he put a bronze helmet on his head and clothed him with a coat of mail. 39 David strapped Saul's sword over the armour, and he tried in vain to walk, for he was not used to them. Then

David said to Saul, "I cannot walk with these; for I am not used to them." So David removed them. 40 Then he took his staff in his hand, and chose five smooth stones from the wadi, and put them in his shepherd's bag, in the pouch; his sling was in his hand, and he drew near to the Philistine. 41 The Philistine came on and drew near to David, with his shield-bearer in front of him. 42 When the Philistine looked and saw David, he disdained him, for he was only a youth, ruddy and handsome in appearance. 43 The Philistine said to David, "Am I a dog, that you come to me with sticks?" And the Philistine cursed David by his gods. 44 The Philistine said to David, "Come to me, and I will give your flesh to the birds of the air and to the wild animals of the field." 45 But David said to the Philistine, "You come to me with sword and spear and javelin; but I come to you in the name of the LORD of hosts, the God of the armies of Israel, whom you have defied. 46 This very day the LORD will deliver you into my hand, and I will strike you down and cut off your head; and I will give the dead bodies of the Philistine army this very day to the birds of the air and to the wild animals of the earth, so that all the earth may know that there is a God in Israel, 47 and that all this assembly may know that the LORD does not save by sword and spear; for the battle is the Lord's and he will give you into our hand." 48 When the Philistine drew nearer to meet David, David ran quickly toward the battle line to meet the Philistine. 49 David put his hand in his bag, took out a stone, slung it, and struck the Philistine on his forehead; the stone sank into his forehead, and he fell face down on the ground. 50 So David prevailed over the Philistine with a sling and a stone, striking down the Philistine and killing him; there was no sword in David's hand. 51 Then David ran and stood over the Philistine; he grasped his sword, drew it out of its sheath, and killed him; then he cut off his head with it. When the Philistines saw that their champion was dead, they fled. 52 The troops of Israel and Judah rose up with a shout and pursued the Philistines as far as Gath and the gates of Ekron, so that the wounded Philistines fell on the way from Shaaraim as far as Gath and Ekron. 53 The Israelites came back from chasing the Philistines, and they plundered their camp. 54 David took the head of the Philistine and brought it to Jerusalem; but he put his armour in his tent.

David and Goliath (Story 1): Veggie tales

CONTEXT

This story was told by a mother (M) to a son (S) aged 5.

DISCUSSION, EXPERIENCE AND COMMENT

The young boy thought the story was good and he recognized it as being the same as that he had on a videotape of "Veggie Tales".

He listened well even though he began to fidget towards the end due to the length of the narrative. The mother was impressed by his ability to link this story to that told by way of cartoon vegetables.

David and Goliath (Story 2): You can be little

CONTEXT

This story was told by a mother (M) to a son aged 10 (S) and a daughter aged 8 (D).

DISCUSSION

M So what is this story about?

S He (David) was brave and he believed in God... Instead of a big sword and weapons, all he has is a little stone and a sling.

D How would he be able to kill him with just a stone?

M He probably got practice from killing bears and lions when his sheep were about to be eaten.

D How big was Goliath?

M Very big. Eight or nine feet. Bigger than most men.

D It teaches you that you don't have to be big and strong to do something brave. You can be little.

S Just because there's a load of stuff against you, it doesn't mean you can't. David used a sling.

D He had a sword and stuff. He had God helping him.

S He believed God would help him because all the other times, if God hadn't been with him, he wouldn't have killed the bear or the lion.

D If you've got a friend with you, you'll win the battle. That's God.

EXPERIENCE

The mother enjoyed this discussion about a well-known story that was enlivened by it being read at source rather than from a children's Bible. She was surprised that the children took the message to be about being small and winning through, only making the link with God at the end of the conversation.

COMMENT

The story of David and Goliath has always been valued by children because they can identify with David as being the little guy in a big world. Things happen to David but he is not dismayed, uses his resources, trusts God and wins through. The technical details in the story are also fascinating as it draws the child to wonder about how a sling weapon and faith in God makes a difference.

The Resurrection of Jesus (John 19 v 13–20 v 25)

(John 19) 13 When Pilate heard these words, he brought Jesus outside and sat on the judge's bench at a place called The Stone Pavement, or in Hebrew Gabbatha. 14 Now it was the day of Preparation for the Passover; and it was about noon. He said to the Jews, "Here is your King!" 15 They cried out, "Away with him! Away with him! Crucify him!" Pilate asked them, "Shall I crucify your King?" The chief priests answered, "We have no king but the emperor." 16 Then he handed him over to them to be crucified.

So they took Jesus; 17 and carrying the cross by himself, he went out to what is called The Place of the Skull, which in Hebrew is called Golgotha. 18 There they crucified him, and with him two others, one on either side, with Jesus between them. 19 Pilate also had an inscription written and put on the cross. It read, "Jesus of Nazareth, the King of the Jews." 20 Many of the Jews read this inscription, because the place where Jesus was crucified was near the city; and it was written in Hebrew, in Latin, and in Greek. 21 Then the chief priests of the Jews said to Pilate, "Do not write, 'The King of the Jews,' but, 'This man said, I am King of the Jews.'" 22 Pilate answered, "What I have written I have written." 23 When the soldiers had crucified Jesus, they took his clothes and divided them into four parts, one for each soldier. They also took his tunic; now the tunic was seamless, woven in one piece from the top. 24 So they said to one another, "Let us not tear it, but cast lots for it to see who will get it." This was to fulfil what the scripture says, "They divided my clothes among themselves, and for my clothing they cast lots." 25 And that is what the soldiers did. Meanwhile, standing near the cross of Jesus were his mother, and his mother's sister, Mary the wife of Clopas, and Mary Magdalene. 26 When Jesus saw his mother and the disciple whom he loved standing beside her, he said to his mother, "Woman, here is your son." 27 Then he said to the disciple, "Here is your mother." And from that hour the disciple took her into his own home. 28 After this, when Jesus knew that all was now finished, he said (in order to fulfil the scripture), "I am thirsty." 29 A jar full of sour wine was standing there. So they put a sponge full of the wine on a branch of hyssop and held it to his mouth. 30 When Jesus had received the wine, he said, "It is finished." Then he bowed his head and gave up his spirit. 31 Since it was the day of Preparation, the Jews did not want the bodies left on the cross during the sabbath, especially because that sabbath was a day of great solemnity. So they asked Pilate to have the legs of the crucified men broken and the bodies removed. 32 Then the soldiers came and broke the legs of the first and of the other who had been crucified with him. 33 But when they came to Jesus and saw that he was already dead, they did not break his legs. 34 Instead, one of the soldiers pierced his side with a spear, and at once blood and water came out. 35 (He who saw this has testified so that you also may believe. His testimony is true, and he knows that he tells the truth.) 36 These things occurred so that the scripture might be fulfilled, "None of his bones shall be broken." 37 And again another passage of scripture says, "They will look on the one whom they have pierced." 38 After these things, Joseph of Arimathea, who was a disciple of Jesus, though a secret one because of his fear of the Jews, asked Pilate to let him take away the body of Jesus. Pilate gave him permission; so he came and removed his body. 39 Nicodemus, who had at first come to Jesus by night, also came, bringing a mixture of myrrh and aloes, weighing about a hundred pounds. 40 They took the body of Jesus and wrapped it with the spices in linen cloths, according to the burial custom of the Jews. 41 Now there was a garden in the place where he was crucified, and in the garden there was a new tomb in which no one had ever been laid. 42 And so, because it was the Jewish day of Preparation, and the tomb was nearby, they laid Jesus there.

(John 20) Early on the first day of the week, while it was still dark, Mary Magdalene came to the tomb and saw that the stone had been removed from the tomb. 2 So she ran and went to Simon Peter and the other disciple, the one whom Jesus loved, and said to them, "They have taken the Lord out of the tomb, and we do not know where they have laid him." 3 Then Peter and the other disciple set out and went toward the tomb. 4 The two were running together, but the other disciple outran Peter and reached the tomb first. 5 He bent down to look in and saw the linen wrappings lying there, but he did not go in. 6 Then Simon Peter came, following him, and went into the tomb. He saw the linen wrappings lying there, 7 and the cloth that had been on Jesus' head, not lying with the linen wrappings but rolled up in a place by itself. 8 Then the other disciple, who reached the tomb first, also went in, and he saw and believed; 9 for as yet they did not understand the scripture, that he must rise from the dead. 10 Then the disciples returned to their homes. 11 But Mary stood weeping outside the tomb. As she wept, she bent over to look into the tomb; 12 and she saw two angels in white, sitting where the body of Jesus had been lying, one at the head and the other at the feet. 13 They said to her, "Woman, why are you weeping?" She said to them, "They have taken away my Lord, and I do not know where they have laid him." 14 When she had said this, she turned around and saw Jesus standing there, but she did not know that it was Jesus. 15 Jesus said to her, "Woman, why are you weeping? Whom are you looking for?" Supposing him to be the gardener, she said to him, "Sir, if you have carried him away, tell me where you have laid him, and I will take him away." 16 Jesus said to her, "Mary!" She turned and said to him in Hebrew, "Rabbuni!" (which means Teacher). 17 Jesus said to her, "Do not hold on to me, because I have not yet ascended to the Father. But go to my brothers and say to them, "I am ascending to my Father and your Father, to my God and your God.""" 18 Mary Magdalene went and announced to the disciples, "I have seen the Lord"; and she told them that he had said these things to her. 19 When it was evening on that day, the first day of the week, and the doors of the house where the disciples had met were locked for fear of the Jews, Jesus came and stood among them and said, "Peace be with you." 20 After he said this, he showed them his hands and his side. Then the disciples rejoiced when they saw the Lord. 21 Jesus said to them again, "Peace be with you. As the Father has sent me, so I send you." 22 When he had said this, he breathed on them and said to them, "Receive the Holy Spirit. 23 If you forgive the sins of any, they are forgiven them; if you retain the sins of any, they are retained." 24 But Thomas (who was called the Twin), one of the twelve, was not with them when Jesus came. 25 So the other disciples told him, "We have seen the Lord." But he said to them, "Unless I see the mark of the nails in his hands, and put my finger in the mark of the nails and my hand in his side, I will not believe."

The Resurrection of Jesus (Story 1): Cloths, spices and angels

CONTEXT

This story was told by a mother (M) to a daughter (D) aged 5.

DISCUSSION

D (Interrupting at 19 v 26 when Jesus' mother is mentioned) How old was Jesus when this happened?

M He was thirty-three years old.

D So where did his mother go after Jesus died?

M She stayed near his body to look after Him.

D (Interrupts at 20 v 15). How did Mary think that Jesus was the gardener?

M Maybe she was crying so much she couldn't see properly.

The conversation continued with the child asking what a tomb was and showing an interest in the cloths and spices. She also talked about the angels, which her mother presumed was because she was cast as an angel on two occasions in Nativity plays.

EXPERIENCE

The mother was encouraged that such a long story could keep the attention of a five-year-old. However, she was surprised that the crucifixion event did not horrify her daughter and she even commented that she was a little disappointed that she did not get a more dramatic response.

COMMENT

This story is unlikely to be horrific to the child because she was familiar with the ending and because this known story has moved from the historic into the devotional. The mother's expectation that more feelings would be aroused is likely to be a projection of her own feelings as someone who has reflected on the story.

The child's interest in the details is therefore of a wondrous and exploratory nature rather than as a quest for meaning.

The Resurrection of Jesus (Story 2): It's true if you believe it

CONTEXT

This story was told by a father (F) to a son aged 7 (S).

DISCUSSION AND EXPERIENCE

The following notes were offered by the father, interlacing his experience with the tone of the conversation, following a direct reading of the text.

S listened to the story the whole way through and very occasionally asked questions when I explained things, but by and large did not comment.

Occasionally he fidgeted a bit, but always returned quickly to the story when another phrase caught his attention. After the story I asked him if he remembered the story and all the details of it – I commented that I hadn't remembered everything, but he simply stated that he had heard it all before, and wouldn't be drawn further! I asked him if he thought the story was true, and he said yes. When I asked him why he couldn't explain himself. However he did agree when I suggested that it was because grown-ups had told him it was true, and that I believed it.

COMMENT

A story is sometimes worth telling and then being left to mature. The mysterious or wonderful do not lend themselves easily to words.

The New Jerusalem (Revelation 20 v 11–22 v 21)

(Revelation 20) 11 Then I saw a great white throne and the one who sat on it; the earth and the heaven fled from his presence, and no place was found for them. 12 And I saw the dead, great and small, standing before the throne, and books were opened. Also another book was opened, the book of life. And the dead were judged according to their works, as recorded in the books. 13 And the sea gave up the dead that were in it, Death and Hades gave up the dead that were in them, and all were judged according to what they had done. 14 Then Death and Hades were thrown into the lake of fire. This is the second death, the lake of fire; 15 and anyone whose name was not found written in the book of life was thrown into the lake of fire.

(Revelation 21) Then I saw a new heaven and a new earth; for the first heaven and the first earth had passed away, and the sea was no more. 2 And I saw the holy city, the new Jerusalem, coming down out of heaven from God, prepared as a bride adorned for her husband. 3 And I heard a loud voice from the throne saying, "See, the home of God is among mortals. He will dwell with them as their God; they will be his peoples, and God himself will be with them; 4 he will wipe every tear from their eyes. Death will be no more; mourning and crying and pain will be no more, for the first things have passed away." 5 And the one who was seated on the throne said, "See, I am making all things new." Also he said, "Write this, for these words are trustworthy and true." 6 Then he said to me, "It is done! I am the Alpha and the Omega, the beginning and the end. To the thirsty I will give water as a gift from the spring of the water of life. 7 Those who conquer will inherit these things, and I will be their God and they will be my children. 8 But as for the cowardly, the faithless, the polluted, the murderers, the fornicators, the sorcerers, the idolaters, and all liars, their place will be in the lake that burns with fire and sulfur, which is the second death." 9 Then one of the seven angels who had the seven bowls full of the seven last plagues came and said to me, "Come, I will show you the bride, the wife of the Lamb." 10 And in the spirit he carried me away to a great, high mountain and showed me the holy city Jerusalem coming down out of heaven from God. 11 It has the glory of God and a radiance like a very rare jewel, like jasper, clear as crystal. 12 It has a great, high wall with twelve gates, and at the gates twelve angels, and on the gates are inscribed the names of the twelve tribes of the Israelites; 13 on the east three gates, on the north three gates, on the south three gates, and on the west three gates. 14 And the wall of the city has twelve foundations, and on them are the twelve names of the twelve apostles of the Lamb. 15 The angel who talked to me had a measuring rod of gold to measure the city and its gates and walls. 16 The city lies foursquare, its length the same as its width; and he measured the city with his rod, fifteen hundred miles; its length and width and height are equal. 17 He also measured its wall, one hundred forty-four cubits by human measurement, which the angel was using. 18 The wall is built of jasper, while the city is pure gold, clear as glass. 19 The foundations of the wall of the city are adorned with every jewel; the first was jasper, the second sapphire, the third agate, the fourth emerald, 20 the fifth onyx, the sixth carnelian, the seventh chrysolite, the eighth beryl, the ninth topaz, the tenth chrysoprase, the eleventh jacinth, the twelfth amethyst. 21 And the twelve gates are twelve pearls, each of the gates is a single pearl, and the street of the city is pure gold, transparent as glass. 22 I saw no temple in the city, for its temple is the Lord God the Almighty and the Lamb. 23 And the city has no need of sun or moon to shine on it, for the glory of God is its light, and its lamp is the Lamb. 24 The nations will walk by its light, and the kings of the earth will bring their glory into it. 25 Its gates will never be shut by day — and there will be no night there. 26 People will bring into it the glory and the honor of the nations. 27 But nothing unclean will enter it, nor anyone who practices abomination or falsehood, but only those who are written in the Lamb's book of life.

(Revelation 22) Then the angel showed me the river of the water of life, bright as crystal, flowing from the throne of God and of the Lamb 2 through the middle of the street of the city. On either side of the river is the tree of life with its twelve kinds of fruit, producing its fruit each month; and the leaves of the tree are for the healing of the nations. 3 Nothing accursed will be found there any more. But the throne of God and of the Lamb will be in it, and his servants will worship him; 4 they will see his face, and his name will be on their foreheads. 5 And there will be no more night; they need no light of lamp or sun, for the Lord God will be their light, and they will reign forever and ever. 6 And he said to me, "These words are trustworthy and true, for the Lord, the God of the spirits of the prophets, has sent his angel to show his servants what must soon take place." 7 "See, I am coming soon! Blessed is the one who keeps the words of the prophecy of this book." 8 I, John, am the one who heard and saw these things. And when I heard and saw them, I fell down to worship at the feet of the angel who showed them to me; 9 but he said to me, "You must not do that! I am a fellow servant with you and your comrades the prophets, and with those who keep the words of this book.

Worship God!" 10 And he said to me, "Do not seal up the words of the prophecy of this book, for the time is near. 11 Let the evil-doer still do evil, and the filthy still be filthy, and the righteous still do right, and the holy still be holy." 12 "See, I am coming soon; my reward is with me, to repay according to everyone's work. 13 I am the Alpha and the Omega, the first and the last, the beginning and the end." 14 Blessed are those who wash their robes, so that they will have the right to the tree of life and may enter the city by the gates. 15 Outside are the dogs and sorcerers and fornicators and murderers and idolaters, and everyone who loves and practices falsehood. 16 "It is I, Jesus, who sent my angel to you with this testimony for the churches. I am the root and the descendant of David, the bright morning star." 17 The Spirit and the bride say, "Come." And let everyone who hears say, "Come." And let every-one who is thirsty come. Let anyone who wishes take the water of life as a gift. 18 I warn everyone who hears the words of the prophecy of this book: if anyone adds to them, God will add to that person the plagues described in this book; 19 if anyone takes away from the words of the book of this prophecy, God will take away that person's share in the tree of life and in the holy city, which are described in this book. 20 The one who testifies to these things says, "Surely I am coming soon." Amen. Come, Lord Jesus! 21 The grace of the Lord Jesus be with all the saints. Amen.

The New Jerusalem (Story 1): Is my name in the Book of Life?
CONTEXT
This story was told by a mother (M) to a daughter (D) aged 7.

DISCUSSION
The daughter has worked out that each time a text is read from a specific genre, the mother is choosing a particular story from one of three. On this occasion she began by asking what other stories were available.

D What stories are we choosing from tonight?

M They are stories that bring comfort and hope. The choice is David and Goliath, The Resurrection of Jesus or the story of The New Jerusalem.

D I know the first two, so let's do the one about the New Jerusalem. (Story is read)

D This is a really long story. What is the "Book of Life?"

M It is the book in which your name is written if you are to live forever.

D Is my name in it?

M Yes… because you have been baptised.

D Is this story true?

M As you know, the Bible is like a library made of many books. These books contain truth but are not necessarily true.

D Is Jesus true?

M Absolutely true.

D I wonder if he is? It would help if I could see him.

EXPERIENCE

The mother did not find this storytelling enjoyable due to the difficult imaging. She felt that despite her considerable learning (she had an MA in theology) this passage was raising more questions than she could answer. She could not help wishing the child had selected one of the other stories on offer.

COMMENT

It seems that the difficulty presenting itself in this encounter is that the mother feels the need to be able to explain the story, to rationalize the various concepts and to defend the faith. Maybe it would be of greater value were she to also respond to the story as a hearer and not only as the defender. We do not own the story.

In this instance, the child is pushing the boundaries of truth and reliability and needs to reflect on what she herself believes and how she believes. Without this, the engagement between parent and child will inevitably lead to a debate where the child tests her faith concepts on the parent who has aligned herself with the faith position. This could be deflected by the parent offering some questions amidst her certainty or by prefacing some of her beliefs with, "This is difficult but I think…" etc.

The New Jerusalem (Story 2): The difficultly with heaven

CONTEXT

This story was told by a father (F) to a daughter (D) aged 10.

DISCUSSION

F How did you get on with this story?

D That was really long and boring. It must be difficult to write about heaven.

F What do you think heaven is like?

D I don't know. I've never thought about it.
   This story says lots of pointless things like how big heaven is or how many gates.

F It also mentions the Book of Life, the book that names the people who go to heaven. Would you like to be in that book?

D Yes (Began to sing a song from the musical "Joseph" that echoed this story).

EXPERIENCE

The father found this passage difficult to read with energy due to the complex sentence structure. He also found the text to be repetitive.

COMMENT

This discussion appears to be lifeless because neither parent nor child is inspired by the text. The father's attempts to get his daughter to imagine heaven or to being registered to go there, do not meet with success because she has not hitherto wondered about it and is not drawn into being imaginative. However, a chink of light is found in the young girl's realization that it must be difficult to write about heaven. It is true she has never thought about it, but after this story, she might.

Chapter 6

Texts of Comedy

Balaam's Ass (Numbers 22 v 21–35)

(Numbers 22) 21 So Balaam got up in the morning, saddled his donkey, and went with the officials of Moab. 22 God's anger was kindled because he was going, and the angel of the LORD took his stand in the road as his adversary. Now he was riding on the donkey, and his two servants were with him. 23 The donkey saw the angel of the LORD standing in the road, with a drawn sword in his hand; so the donkey turned off the road, and went into the field; and Balaam struck the donkey, to turn it back onto the road. 24 Then the angel of the LORD stood in a narrow path between the vineyards, with a wall on either side. 25 When the donkey saw the angel of the LORD, it scraped against the wall, and scraped Balaam's foot against the wall; so he struck it again. 26 Then the angel of the LORD went ahead, and stood in a narrow place, where there was no way to turn either to the right or to the left. 27 When the donkey saw the angel of the LORD, it lay down under Balaam; and Balaam's anger was kindled, and he struck the donkey with his staff. 28 Then the LORD opened the mouth of the donkey, and it said to Balaam, "What have I done to you, that you have struck me these three times?" 29 Balaam said to the donkey, "Because you have made a fool of me! I wish I had a sword in my hand! I would kill you right now!" 30 But the donkey said to Balaam, "Am I not your donkey, which you have ridden all your life to this day? Have I been in the habit of treating you this way?" And he said, "No." 31 Then the LORD opened the eyes of Balaam, and he saw the angel of the LORD standing in the road, with his drawn sword in his hand; and he bowed down, falling on his face. 32 The angel of the LORD said to him, "Why have you struck your donkey these three times? I have come out as an adversary, because your way is perverse before me. 33 The donkey saw me, and turned away from me these three times. If it had not turned away from me, surely just now I would have killed you and let it live." 34 Then Balaam said to the angel of the LORD, "I have sinned, for I did not know that you were standing in the road to oppose me. Now therefore, if it is displeasing to you, I will return home." 35 The angel of the LORD said to Balaam, "Go with the men; but speak only what I tell you to speak." So Balaam went on with the officials of Balak.

Balaam's Ass (Story 1): Do angels kills good people?

CONTEXT

This story was told by a mother (M) to a son (S) aged 5.

DISCUSSION

S That's a funny story. I liked the angel. They're good. (pause) Why did the angel have a sword?

M Why do you think?

S I think it is because the angel can fight. Does he kill good people?

M I don't think so.

EXPERIENCE

The mother was intrigued by her son's fascination with angels in this story. He peppered her reading of it by frequent comments about angels to the extent that he could not even be distracted onto the subject of a talking donkey.

COMMENT

The child might equally have become fixated by the talking donkey as by the angel, in that both occupy that zone interfacing reality and imagination.

Children are fascinated by angels and a child of five will be at a stage of development that Fowler (1981) would call "mythic-literalism". It is that phase where the permanent objects and non-permanent objects are classified. In this instance, an angel will exist as an object that belongs to both the permanent and the non-permanent worlds, as the angel occupies the interface between the spiritual and the material. As such they are beloved by children. Further insights into how key stage two children (aged 8–11) understand angels is offered in Worsley 2009.

Balaam's Ass (Story 2): Adversaries

CONTEXT

This story was told by a mother (M) to a daughter (D) aged 7.

DISCUSSION

During the telling of this story, the child asked for clarification of difficult words.

D What does adversary mean?

M It means that someone is your opponent. Here, the angel of the Lord is standing against Balaam to block his way.

D A bit like in karate?

M Yes, a bit like that.

D In karate your opponent might still be your friend even if you spar with them.

M Yes… though here the angel says to Balaam that he is his adversary because his way is perverse.

D What does perverse mean?

M It means that Balaam is on the wrong path and that he is doing wrong.

D I think that this story was not written in English. The writer could have used better words. Why say "adversary" when you mean "opponent" or "perverse" when you mean "wrong"?

EXPERIENCE

This discussion over language was surprising to the mother because her daughter normally likes to learn new vocabulary.

Because the conversation concerned the meaning of words it did not look into the context whereby the donkey spoke and God showed anger. This was a relief to the mother who found these concepts difficult and who was worried that her misgivings might have been shown.

COMMENT

Language is a powerful tool whereby we learn to control our environment and it is here that the child wishes to focus her attention on this occasion. She takes out her irritation on not fully grasping the details of the story by criticizing the particular use of language.

The mother's difficulties over the concepts prevent her from defending the faith in her answers.

Balaam's Ass (Story 3): Just like Shrek

CONTEXT

This story was told by a mother (M) to a daughter (D) aged 10.

DISCUSSION

D That was a wonderful story about a clever donkey. He was just like Shrek.

M What is it you like about it?

D It's a funny story and the most important person is the donkey. He is clever and can talk.

M So you liked this Bible story?

D Yes, but it's not from the Bible.

M It is. Let me show you. (She gets out the children's Bible and shows the story in the main volume.)

EXPERIENCE

The mother expected her daughter to ask the meaning of some words in the story earlier on. However, when she just listened to the storytelling without requesting clarification, the mother checked and was told that she did not know the meaning of "kindle" or "adversary" but that it did not matter.

The mother expected this story to go down well since "Shrek" was one of her daughter's favourite films. She noted that the donkey so engaged her attention that she failed to be worried about the cruelty of Balaam.

COMMENT

This storytelling clearly depicts two very different worldviews. On the one hand the mother is interested in the education of her child and for her daughter to understand the meaning of the story or of precise words. On the other hand, the child is captivated by the appearance of a talking donkey in a story, so much so that she cannot believe it comes from the Bible. Maybe she has not learnt to view the possibility of stories from the Bible as having a comic element because they have been brought to her only in other, more serious ways.

Balaam's Ass (Story 4): Who had the stretchiest bum in the Bible?

CONTEXT

This story was told by a father (F) to a son aged 7 (A) and a son aged 4 (B). Mother (M) looks on.

DISCUSSION AND EXPERIENCE

The following notes were offered by the father, interlacing his experience with the tone of the conversation following an ad-lib account of the story.

F I enjoyed telling the story – the boys listened very carefully, and joined in a discussion at the end. I used the traditional title, Balaam's Ass, but had to explain that it was about a donkey. I found it difficult to justify Balaam hitting the donkey, and pointed out that this was wrong. I found myself using the story to moralize more than the text actually suggested.

B didn't laugh – he didn't like all the "naughtiness" in the story.

A laughed and enjoyed the story, but agreed he didn't like the naughty behaviour.

When the boys were asked what they would have done if they were the donkey, B said if he got stuck he would go through the trees or hedges and A agreed.

The boys wanted to know how God had made the donkey talk – was it a magic trick?

At the end I told them it was from the Bible and A said he thought so, because it was about God.

M commented that the story reminded us of Pinocchio.

It also reminded everyone of a familiar joke – Who had the stretchiest bum in the Bible? Moses, because he tied his ass to a tree and walked ten miles.

COMMENT

Young children can be strongly moralistic. Their words are governed by law keepers in the form of parents or teachers and so they may simply engage with whether something is naughty (and not allowed) or good (and permissible).

The older son here is beginning to reflect on a wider morality and perceives the humour of the passage.

The comedy surrounding the word "ass" is of course the funniest concept for these boys still remembering their victory over toilet training. The father's explanation that an ass is a donkey and his familiar joke will be a key source of amusement to the children and will keep them engaged with this story for long years to come – because he has crossed over into the "naughty world" in telling them a Bible story.

The Unjust Judge (Luke 18 v 1–8)

(Luke 18) Then Jesus told them a parable about their need to pray always and not to lose heart. 2 He said, "In a certain city there was a judge who neither feared God nor had respect for people. 3 In that city there was a widow who kept coming to him and saying,

'Grant me justice against my opponent.' 4 For a while he refused; but later he said to himself, 'Though I have no fear of God and no respect for anyone, 5 yet because this widow keeps bothering me, I will grant her justice, so that she may not wear me out by continually coming.' 6 And the Lord said, 'Listen to what the unjust judge says. 7 And will not God grant justice to his chosen ones who cry to him day and night? Will he delay long in helping them? 8 I tell you, he will quickly grant justice to them."

The Unjust Judge (Story 1): Why won't that man listen to that woman?

CONTEXT

This story was told by a mother (M) to a daughter (D) aged 5.

DISCUSSION

D Why won't that man listen to that woman?

M We don't know why. Maybe he was busy or maybe a bit lazy. But he was not a very good judge.

D That's not good. Are judges like that nowadays?

M Sometimes, but their job is to do what is right and make good judgements, like God.

D That is why we pray to God isn't it?

M Yes… (pause)… Are there things we could ask God about tonight?

D Pray for school that it is nice … and pray for nice dreams.

EXPERIENCE

The mother recorded that she needed to read this story several times before the session to make sure she was clear in her mind about what she thought it was saying.

Her own understanding was that the message was about persevering in prayer even when it was difficult to do so. This triggered her to praying more herself and to thinking about how to pray more effectively.

COMMENT

This session depicts an occasion where the mother was stimulated by the discussion to think more deeply about the passage and the nature of prayer. She found her daughter's simple reactions a resource to this process.

The Unjust Judge (Story 2): Try, try and try again

CONTEXT

This story was told by a father (F) to a son aged 10 (S) and a daughter aged 8 (D).

DISCUSSION

F What do you think this story means?

S That God will give justice straight away.

D Or is it try, try and try again?

S No, it is that God will give justice fairly and not just to shut you up.

EXPERIENCE

The father recorded that it was an enjoyable storytelling occasion.

COMMENT

This straightforward dialogue leaves no question as to whether the young lad had understood. He feels that the code has been cracked and the message has been laid bare. However, his sister wants to probe in a different way and she follows another line of enquiry, wondering if in fact God wants persistence. Of course, both children are right. The period of questioning has not yet arrived whereby they might ask, "Is God always just?" or "People pray a lot but don't get an answer."

This stage of development (Key stage two, aged 7–11) has been called by some "the age of the young scientist" in that it is a time when things are either right or wrong. It is also a period of considerable spiritual awareness.

The Unjust Judge (Story 3): What does justice stand for?
CONTEXT

This story was told by a mother (M) to a son (S) aged 6.

DISCUSSION

Before the storytelling took place (as usual after bath, sitting on parents' bed before bedtime) the child asked if the story was "for the project." He was pleased that it was. As before, he punctuated the reading of this story with questions and comments.

S (At v 2) (Commenting on a judge who neither feared God nor had respect for people) That's bad!

M (At v 3) Do you know what a widow is?

S Yes. It's like if dad dies, you'd be one.

M And do you know what it would be like to be a widow?

S Yes. Very sad, and you'd be poor. What does she mean when she says "Grant me justice against my opponent?"

M Injustice is like when you are blamed for what you did not do... like when you get told off by the teacher and it's not your fault. Justice is when it's sorted. An opponent is someone who is against you. For the widow it might have been an unjust landlord charging her money.

S So what does justice stand for?

M Justice is about being fair and putting wrong things right!

S So the judge only does it because the widow bothers him. He's not really nice is he?

M No, he's the opposite of God. God always acts justly.

EXPERIENCE

On this occasion, the mother prayed with her son before reading the story, asking God to help him understand it. She enjoyed the mother–son interaction and felt he was listening carefully even though she was struggling to find a practical application other than to remind him of God's just character.

COMMENT

The mother's experience is key to explaining this storytelling. She has perceived the occasion to be a time to educate her son into spiritual ways and has prayed beforehand and endeavoured to draw out a Christian message. Commendable as this may be, it detracts from the simple enjoyment of storytelling and makes it more of an educational task. The mother's role has become that of the nurturing faith educator and the son's is that of a student. This experience will probably draw out cognitive skills more than imaginative enjoyment. The humour of the passage, or the child's wonder are some of the aspects that are not noted in this engagement.

The Seven Husbands in Heaven (Luke 20 v 27–40)

27 Some Sadducees, those who say there is no resurrection, came to him 28 and asked him a question, "Teacher, Moses wrote for us that if a man's brother dies, leaving a wife but no children, the man shall marry the widow and raise up children for his brother. 29 Now there were seven brothers; the first married, and died childless; 30 then the second 31 and the third married her, and so in the same way all seven died childless. 32 Finally the woman also died. 33 In the resurrection, therefore, whose wife will the woman be? For the seven had married her." 34 Jesus said to them, "Those who belong to this age marry and are given in marriage; 35 but those who are considered worthy of a place in that age and in the resurrection from the dead neither marry nor are given in marriage. 36 Indeed they cannot die anymore, because they are like angels and are children of God, being children of the resurrection. 37 And the fact that the dead are raised Moses himself showed, in the story about the bush, where he speaks of the Lord as the God of Abraham, the God of Isaac, and the God of Jacob. 38 Now he is God not of the dead, but of the living; for to him all of them are alive." 39 Then some of the scribes answered, "Teacher, you have spoken well." 40 For they no longer dared to ask him another question.

The Seven Husbands in Heaven (Story 1): The smelly guy and the attractive woman

CONTEXT

This story was told by a father (F) to two teenage sons aged 17 (A) and 14 (B).

DISCUSSION

The boys asked for this story to be read twice over as they thought the story was more complex than at first hearing.

B Why did they (the Sadducees) ask about something they don't believe in? (Referring to the resurrection)

A They are trying to trick Jesus. They're mocking him.

B I don't get why they don't believe in the resurrection. The Old Testament talks about it.

F Does it?

B Maybe not! Is it just the New Testament?

A Well in the Old Testament Elijah goes into heaven in a chariot and Elishah raises a boy to life.

F OK. Good connections, but does this mean that belief in the resurrection was normal in the Old Testament?

A I'll come back to you on that. Can we get back to the story?

B It's weird, the idea of marrying your brother's wife if he dies!

A This was a different culture. I'm not sure I find Jesus' answer very satisfactory. It feels flippant. He might be being humorous but he does not relate the story to human emotions and experiences. It's a frightening story. It's beyond us.

F Why is it frightening?

A We only know relationships that have a hope of a future, that are interdependent. To think of a time when there is no marriage is alien. It does not feel human.

F Is this a literal story?

A I'm not sure what Jesus is saying. I've heard preachers at Church use this to say that there's no marriage in heaven literally but I don't know. This is the problem with a flat story… there's no tone. I can't hear if Jesus is being comical or serious. If he's serious, he's being literal. If he's comical, he's taking the rise.

B What if one of the brothers was a little, bald, smelly guy and she was dead attractive? That's funny!

F Yes. So Jesus is telling a funny story?

A No. This story is ambiguous. It can be interpreted in many ways.

B Who wrote it?

F Luke.

A I don't like it. It's not clear.

B Had Jesus told them (the Sadducees) that he was the Son of God?

F No. He never says so anywhere in so many words.

B Yes he did. That's why he was killed.

A He was killed because he never denied that he was the Son of God.

B Why do we believe that he was?

A Because he implied that he was.

B This is complicated.

The conversation then went on to consider how Jesus realized that he was the Son of God and how the early church and Bible writers came up with the understanding that Jesus was both God and man.

A general theory of developmental understanding was suggested in that the boys believed that Jesus gradually realised who he was and that the disciples were a few steps behind that, and the New Testament writers a few steps behind them.

EXPERIENCE

The father was surprised that such a short and humorous story should arouse such strong feelings and complex thoughts. He noted that to range in discussion from Jewish belief in the resurrection to Jesus' perception of himself as divine by way of whether there is marriage in heaven, was both stimulating and exhausting.

COMMENT

To children in a secure family home, the idea that Jesus is not defending eternal marriage is likely to be a difficult one. Within a strong Christian home, the institution of marriage will be something that is defended vigorously and therefore this story comes as a challenge in that Jesus suggests marriage is temporal.

Interestingly, this is more of a threat to the older boy whereas the younger is quicker to pick up on the comedy of the story. It is the younger son who imaginatively pictures the widow as "dead attractive" and at least one of the brothers as being "little, bald and smelly." He also visualizes himself as the younger brother marrying his dead brother's cast-off wife.

So, is the story comical or serious? Maybe the theologizing about wider issues is a deflection from what feels quite frightening and threatening to this family hearthside.

Chapter 7

Texts of Mercy and Forgiveness

Jonah (Jonah 1 & 3–4)

(Jonah 1) Now the word of the LORD came to Jonah son of Amittai, saying, 2 "Go at once to Nineveh, that great city, and cry out against it; for their wickedness has come up before me." 3 But Jonah set out to flee to Tarshish from the presence of the LORD. He went down to Joppa and found a ship going to Tarshish; so he paid his fare and went on board, to go with them to Tarshish, away from the presence of the LORD. 4 But the LORD hurled a great wind upon the sea, and such a mighty storm came upon the sea that the ship threatened to break up. 5 Then the mariners were afraid, and each cried to his god. They threw the cargo that was in the ship into the sea, to lighten it for them. Jonah, meanwhile, had gone down into the hold of the ship and had lain down, and was fast asleep. 6 The captain came and said to him, "What are you doing sound asleep? Get up, call on your god! Perhaps the god will spare us a thought so that we do not perish." 7 The sailors said to one another, "Come, let us cast lots, so that we may know on whose account this calamity has come upon us." So they cast lots, and the lot fell on Jonah. 8 Then they said to him, "Tell us why this calamity has come upon us. What is your occupation? Where do you come from? What is your country? And of what people are you?" 9 "I am a Hebrew," he replied. "I worship the LORD, the God of heaven, who made the sea and the dry land." 10 Then the men were even more afraid, and said to him, "What is this that you have done!" For the men knew that he was fleeing from the presence of the LORD, because he had told them so. 11 Then they said to him, "What shall we do to you, that the sea may quiet down for us?" For the sea was growing more and more tempestuous. 12 He said to them, "Pick me up and throw me into the sea; then the sea will quiet down for you; for I know it is because of me that this great storm has come upon you." 13 Nevertheless the men rowed hard to bring the ship back to land, but they could not, for the sea grew more and more stormy against them. 14 Then they cried out to the LORD, "Please, O LORD, we pray, do not let us perish on account of this man's life. Do not make us guilty of innocent blood; for you, O LORD, have done as it pleased you." 15 So they picked Jonah up and threw him into the sea; and the sea ceased from its raging. 16 Then the men feared the LORD even more, and they offered a sacrifice to the LORD and made vows. 17 But the LORD provided a large fish to swallow up Jonah; and Jonah was in the belly of the fish three days and three nights.

(Jonah 3) The word of the LORD came to Jonah a second time, saying, 2 "Get up, go to Nineveh, that great city, and proclaim to it the message that I tell you." 3 So Jonah set out and went to Nineveh, according to the word of the LORD. Now Nineveh was an exceedingly large city, a three days' walk across. 4 Jonah began to go into the city, going a day's walk. And he cried out, "Forty days more, and Nineveh shall be overthrown!" 5 And the people of Nineveh believed God; they proclaimed a fast, and everyone, great and small, put on sackcloth. 6 When the news reached the king of Nineveh, he rose from his throne, removed his robe, covered himself with sackcloth, and sat in ashes. 7 Then he had a proclamation made in Nineveh: "By the decree of the king and his nobles: No human being or animal, no herd or flock, shall taste anything. They shall not feed, nor shall they drink water. 8 Human beings and animals shall be covered with sackcloth, and they shall cry mightily to God. All shall turn from their evil ways and from the violence that is in their hands. 9 Who knows? God may relent and change his mind; he may turn from his fierce anger, so that we do not perish." 10 When God saw what they did, how they turned from their evil ways, God changed his mind about the calamity that he had said he would bring upon them; and he did not do it.

(Jonah 4) But this was very displeasing to Jonah, and he became angry. 2 He prayed to the LORD and said, "O LORD! Is not this what I said while I was still in my own country? That is why I fled to Tarshish at the beginning; for I knew that you are a gracious God and merciful, slow to anger, and abounding in steadfast love, and ready to relent from punishing. 3 And now, O LORD, please take my life from me, for it is better for me to die than to live." 4 And the LORD said, "Is it right for you to be angry?" 5 Then Jonah went out of the city and sat down east of the city, and made a booth for himself there. He sat under it in the shade, waiting to see what would become of the city. 6 The LORD God appointed a bush, and made it come up over Jonah, to give shade over his head, to save him from his discomfort; so Jonah was very happy about the bush. 7 But when dawn came up the next day, God appointed a worm that attacked the bush, so that it withered. 8 When the sun rose, God prepared a sultry east wind, and the sun beat down on the head of Jonah so that he was faint and asked that he might die. He said, "It is better for me to die than to live." 9 But God said to Jonah, "Is it right for you to be angry about the bush?" And he said, "Yes, angry enough to die." 10 Then the LORD said, "You are concerned about the bush, for which you did not labour and which you did not grow; it came into being in a night and perished in a night. 11 And should I not be concerned about Nineveh, that great city, in which there are more than a hundred and twenty thousand persons who do not know their right hand from their left, and also many animals?"

Jonah (Story 1): You've missed the best bit out?

CONTEXT

This story was told by a mother (M) to a daughter (D) aged 10.

DISCUSSION

M Which story would you like tonight; the story of Jonah, the Prodigal Son or the story of Zacchaeus?

D Is the prodigal son the one about the man who ends up feeding pigs and comes home and they have a big party?

M Yes, that's right.

S OK, let's have Jonah.
(Reading of story during which she asks the meaning of "casting lots" and "booth")

D (at the end) You've missed the best bits out. You didn't mention Jonah being spat out of the whale. Anyway, why did God send a bush to cover Jonah and then destroy it? It's pointless!

EXPERIENCE

The mother found the language of this story somewhat archaic and therefore difficult to read. She was interested at her daughter noticing that part of the story was missing (the extract includes Chapters 1, 3 and 4 but omits Chapter 2).

COMMENT

This storytelling event has a less than satisfactory feel to it. This may be because the story of Jonah, popularly told, is high in drama and with a fast-moving plot. This expectation has not been fulfilled, with a more difficult text being used that has been noted to have missed the child's favourite bit – namely Jonah being vomited onto a beach.

Even though the lesser known subplot of the bush that appears and disappears is included, this provides little interest to the child. It is noteworthy that although the bush subplot is similar to the fish main plot in that it shows God being firm with Jonah and then changing His mind, the child is dissatisfied with God's actions in the subplot. Maybe this is a story that should be told with more tragic-comedy to bring out its full effect.

The Prodigal Son (Luke 15 v 11–32)

(Luke 15) 11 Then Jesus said, "There was a man who had two sons. 12 The younger of them said to his father, "Father, give me the share of the property that will belong to me." So he divided his property between them. 13 A few days later the younger son gathered all he had and traveled to a distant country, and there he squandered his property in dissolute living. 14 When he had spent everything, a severe famine took place throughout that country, and he began to be in need. 15 So he went and hired himself out to one of the citizens of that country, who sent him to his fields to feed the pigs. 16 He would gladly have filled himself with the pods that the pigs were eating; and no one gave him anything. 17 But when he came to himself he said, "How many of my father's hired hands have bread enough and to spare, but here I am dying of hunger! 18 I will get up and go to my father, and I will say to him, 'Father, I have sinned against heaven and before you; 19 I am no longer worthy to be called your son; treat me like one of your hired hands.' 20 So he set off and went to his father. But while he was still far off, his father saw him and was filled with compassion; he ran and put his arms around him and kissed him. 21 Then the son said to him, "Father, I have sinned against heaven and before you; I am no longer worthy to be called your son." 22 But the father said to his slaves, "Quickly, bring out a robe – the best one – and put it on him; put a ring on his finger and sandals on his feet. 23 And get the fatted calf and kill it, and let us eat and celebrate; 24 for this son of mine was dead and is alive again; he was lost and is found!" And they began to celebrate. 25 "Now his elder son was in the field; and when he came and approached the house, he heard music and dancing. 26 He called one of the slaves and asked what was going on. 27 He replied, 'Your brother has come, and your father has killed the fatted calf, because he has got him back safe and sound.' 28 Then he became angry and refused to go in. His father came out and began to plead with him. 29 But he answered his father, 'Listen! For all these years I have been working like a slave for you, and I have never disobeyed your command; yet you have never given me even a young goat so that I might celebrate with my friends. 30 But when this son of yours came back, who has devoured your property with prostitutes, you killed the fatted calf for him!' 31 Then the father said to him, 'Son, you are always with me, and all that is mine is yours. 32 But we had to celebrate and rejoice, because this brother of yours was dead and has come to life; he was lost and has been found.'"

The Prodigal Son (Story 1): The younger son is best 'coz he had a party

CONTEXT

This story was told by a father (F) to a son aged 7 (A) and a son aged 4 (B).

DISCUSSION AND EXPERIENCE

The following notes were offered by the father, interlacing his experience with the tone of the conversation, following an ad-lib account of the story.

F Reading the story in advance reminded me of a number of things about the story that I had not remembered – the ring, the famine, the goat, the fact that the story of the prodigal son himself takes up only half the text. (I always think of the elder son as a bit of an after-thought, but actually he takes up just as much of the text.) The main difficulty with the story was explaining the idea of inheritance to the boys, although they accepted my explanation very easily.

A and **B** were not familiar with the title "prodigal" although A recognized the story when I told him. They both wanted to know what "prodigal" meant – I struggled to answer!

Both boys listened carefully to the story. When I said that the younger son ran out of money, A offered "Well, he would, wouldn't he?" He also giggled at the elder son's indignation. Other than that the boys did not interrupt the story.

After the story I explained to the boys that even though we do things that upset God, God always welcomes us back because he loves us.

I asked the boys which of the sons they would have liked to be. A said he would like to be the younger son, because he had a party. B then said he wanted to be the older son, because A had said he wanted to be the younger son!

COMMENT

There can be no doubt that the younger son had the best deal in this story. To get an older son to admit this in the presence of a younger brother makes this point clear.

And of course, the younger son wants to be the older one.

Zacchaeus (Luke 19 v 1–10)

(Luke 19) He entered Jericho and was passing through it. 2 A man was there named Zacchaeus; he was a chief tax collector and was rich. 3 He was trying to see who Jesus was, but on account of the crowd he could not, because he was short in stature. 4 So he ran ahead and climbed a sycamore tree to see him, because he was going to pass that way. 5 When Jesus came to the place, he looked up and said to him, "Zacchaeus, hurry and come down; for I must stay at your house today." 6 So he hurried down and was happy to welcome him. 7 All who saw it began to grumble and said, "He has gone to be the guest of one who is a sinner." 8 Zacchaeus stood there and said to the Lord, "Look, half of my possessions, Lord, I will give to the poor; and if I have defrauded anyone of anything, I will pay back four times as much." 9 Then Jesus said to him, "Today salvation has come to this house, because he too is a son of Abraham. 10 For the Son of Man came to seek out and to save the lost."

Zacchaeus (Story 1): Jesus knew he was a good man

CONTEXT

This story was told by a mother (M) to a son (S) aged 5.

DISCUSSION

S   This is a very, very, very good story. I liked it very much.

M   What did you like?

S   I liked it that Jesus saw Zacchaeus hiding in the tree. He wanted to have his dinner with him.

M   Why did Jesus want to do that?

S   Jesus knew he was a good man, even though the people didn't.

EXPERIENCE

The mother was carried away by her son's enjoyment in this story. Not only was she drawn into his delight but she benefited from his perception that Jesus could see immediately that Zacchaeus was a good man. The insight that God looks deeper than the human eye and is willing to forgive was a refreshing reminder to her.

COMMENT

The simplicity of the story of Zacchaeus is of great value for all-age engagement. A young child is able to engage with the main character who is short and who climbs trees like a child. A teenager is able to empathize with the issues of rejection taking place between the crowds and the offensive tax collector while the adult can reflect on the nature of Christ's discernment, God's forgiveness and the relationship between repentances and repayment.

In this encounter, the child's simple perception of the salient story proves to be a resource to the adult.

Zacchaeus (Story 2): A happy ending

CONTEXT

This story was told by a mother (M) to a daughter (D) aged 5.

DISCUSSION

D This story has a happy ending.

M Yes, it's a good story.

D What was Zacchaeus' job as a tax collector?

M He had to collect taxes from people. That means that he had to collect money for the government.

D That's not bad is it?

M No. The reason he was a bit bad was because he was not very honest and took extra money for himself.

D So it was really nice that Jesus wanted to be his friend and to go to his house?

M Absolutely.

D Being sorry and sorting things out is good.

EXPERIENCE

Both mother and daughter enjoyed this story. The language, the concepts and the meaning were all comfortable to both. The mother noted that she had become very familiar with the story and felt quite humbled to see it again through a child's eyes. She recorded, "The concepts of sin, forgiveness and salvation can all be heavy topics and it was lovely to appreciate the comfort which the story gives. It made me want to explore more stories like this and to rediscover them in a fresh way."

COMMENT

The process of telling this story has clearly been resourceful to both mother and daughter in this instance. For the daughter it has meant the development of concepts, deeper understanding and a resolution. For the mother it has meant the reminder of forgotten concepts and the enlivenment of the power of the Christian meta-narrative (i,e, the narrative linking all other narratives).

Zacchaeus (Story 3): God entering your soul
CONTEXT

This story was told by a mother (M) to a son aged 10 (S) and a daughter aged 8 (D).

DISCUSSION

M What do you think this story means?

S It's about Zacchaeus wanting to give to the poor because he realized he'd sinned. Before that he didn't want to 'cos he was a sinner who kept his money — not like the old lady who gave all she had.

D Also, it's about Zacchaeus wanting to see who the Saviour was.

M How did he know who the Saviour was?

D Everyone was talking about him.

S The story is a lesson. The message is, "If you find out you've sinned, show that you know it."

D Yeah, by letting Jesus come to your house. Jesus coming to his house was like God entering his soul.

EXPERIENCE

This session got off to a slow pace after the mother had tempted her son away from the television. She was very surprised (and amused) by her daughter's comment about Jesus entering Zacchaeus' soul.

COMMENT

This discussion has centred on meaning because that is what was asked for. It is interesting to notice the overlay of meaning that has come from the wider Church context in terms of Zacchaeus being a sinner. The son mentioned sin in both his answers and understood the story to be about making amends for sin. This young man is also able to reference the story with the parable of the widow's mite, evidencing his growing Christian nurture and culture.

Chapter 8

Implications for All Storytellers with Children

All stories originally come from sources that were oral, if traced back far enough. Therefore to tell them aloud is to redeem something of their ancient past. Bible stories originated within communities that found their meaning by the retelling of the narrative, some of which drew on ancient mythical echoes and some of which reworked more recent legends and history. When read aloud to children, Bible stories create a world of imagination and of wonder where faith can grow. If this is done in a way which allows for questions and doubt as well as for affirmation and confirmation of thoughts, the resultant faith will be well-founded, neither diseased by the need to be certain nor choked by the fear of using a creative imagination.

When people of faith have wanted to pass on their religious traditions to their children, they have created rituals as they have retold the story. Setting his pen to parchment a thousand years before Christ, the psalmist wrote,

> *Give ear, O my people to my teaching,*
> *Incline your ears to the words of my mouth.*
> *I will open my mouth in a parable,*
> *I will utter dark sayings from of old,*
> *Things that we have heard and known,*

That our ancestors have told us.
We will not hide them from our children;
We will tell them to the coming generation,
The glorious deeds of the Lord and his might,
And the wonders that he has done. (Psalm 78 v 1–4)

The same psalm goes on to say that the reason for telling the stories of the tradition is that future generations of children would hope in God.

The telling of Bible stories to children is in this long line of tradition and the way in which it is done today is likely to develop its own rituals. Most families made the time for telling stories just before going to bed at night, a time when there was time to both listen to the story and also to engage with the ideas and wrestle with the concepts. In a few instances where parents have told stories to children under the age of 5, they have done so at a quieter part of the day, at a time when the child is less active and more reflective. In one family in this sample, the practice of telling stories that began when the children were very small, continued to be a ritual that lasted through the whole of secondary education and continued as a custom when the family reconvened after the older ones had gone to university.

The benefits of such storytelling are immense, both in homes where the faith tradition is important and in places where there is simply an interest in developing spirituality (which may or may not be religious). The resourcefulness of such practice is discussed in terms of implications for children, parents, school teachers and Church ministers.

Implications for children

At the time of writing, a United Nations report is being widely discussed in its comments that British children are amongst the least contented children on the planet. There is a sense that children are not being well-served by the educational system. There is also a suggestion that children are having insufficient time with their parents, particularly with their fathers.

The practice of telling stories to children is something that bucks these trends. On an educational level, storytelling allows the child to engage with a wider range of language and to become aware of the power of the narrative. Attention spans and concentration are strengthened by the art of listening. So too is the ability to ask questions, to reflect, to find one's own opinions and to converse.

Probably the most important thing is that storytelling demands time and involves the establishment of a space that is sacrosanct. Into this zone, the child can relax and enjoy the security of parent time, a period when certain rituals are observed and when a deeper processing can take place. Children who can rely on this custom will be those who are better resourced educationally, spiritually and in terms of their own security.

If certain rules are kept, the moment of storytelling can be made doubly fertile. Those rules are:

1. **The regularity of the occasion.** Storytelling need not take place every night but it probably needs to happen at least weekly.

2. **The importance of the occasion.** Whoever is involved, both teller and listener, needs to think about it, anticipate it and come prepared.

3. **The timing of the occasion.** Because storytelling is important, it will be a feature in the parents' day and will be known by the child as well. Not only will it be clear as to when the story starts but it will be known how much time is available.

4. **The ambience of the occasion.** As with any special moment, the ritual can be enhanced by attention being given to lighting,

heat, sound or smell, as well as by a particular room or chair. It can be further augmented on occasions by food or drink.

5. **The sacredness of the occasion.** Storytelling is a time that is not to be interrupted by the telephone nor invaded by any other person unless consultation has taken place. I was amused to hear one parent saying that he'd kept an important visitor waiting in another room whilst he concluded a story. On this occasion the visitor had been half an hour early for a meeting and the parent had not sacrificed the storytime but had made his guest comfortable and returned to his covenanted story.

6. **The internal engagement of the occasion**. All families will have their own rules of engagement, but a general rule is that the story should be told with occasional interruption. If there is no interruption, then the complex issues of comprehension or discussion are all left to the end and may be forgotten.

   If interruption takes place too frequently, the story may never gather momentum and if the group involves more than one child, it may cause frustration. Some sort of balance is required to allow the story to be the focus.

After the story has been told, the conversation needs to allow for adequate reflection and wonder in which both storyteller and listeners respond to the story. At this point the parent needs to be careful not to take the role of priest or guardian of the story by defending every aspect that has been told. If they fall into this trap, they will stifle the child's freedom to criticize and imply a need for them to accept the story without rigorous engagement. If the parent can find a place as being "beneath the story" then they can offer reflection alongside the child whereby they too are in a place of wonder, not of proclamation.

Implications for parents

When these six hallmarks of good storytelling are evident, the story is released and will be effective. Of course the story may often contain aspects that are unresolved, that are uncomfortable or are frankly sinister. Such is the case with the "texts of terror".

When this is the case, the parent may need to offer more protection, depending on the age of the child, and whether they need to distance themselves from the possible interpretation of the story. For example, after the reading of "Abraham and Isaac" or "Jephthah's Return", it may be important to say, "I would never sacrifice you in any situation. This story comes from a long time ago when people had different ideas."

However, the parent should not be overly anxious about the dark strands in a story, as it is these that intrigue the child in a secure environment and which are the focus for on-going discussion and learning. As Bettelheim has demonstrated in *The Uses of Enchantment* (1976), where he discussed the sinister themes in fairy stories, it is these strands that help add a true context and meaning for the child. Children need to be aware that the outside world can be hostile and can threaten their safety and there is no better place to grapple with this than in the sacred space of storytelling.

This is Vygotsky's Zone of proximal development (1962) – a place where the child faces the darkness from the security of the parent's arms and from a known place. This is where the child can reflect that Hansel is able to fool the shortsighted witch who tries to fatten him up, by having the cunning to offer a dry bone instead of a finger through the bars of his cage. Far from being a horror story, Hansel and Gretel is a story of adventure and survival as children learn to live outside of the family home.

It is the same with issues of faith in that religion offers a meta-narrative to explain the complexities of the story of how the world works. The meta-narrative offers meaning, but the meaning is not complete in that it will hold out a hope for the eschatological future whilst making sense of the past (eschatological future being the study of the last times, in other words the Christian narrative spans the past, the present and the future, adding connectivity and meaning to all). That is one of the reasons why religions tell stories, because stories are able to maintain the present in dynamic tension between what has been and what is yet to come.

When the child engages with the Christian story and moves towards a position of personal faith, this will happen because they have been free to own faith and not because they have been trapped into having no other options of belief. If the growing child is nurtured within the closed world of religious certainty, then the danger is that he or she might develop a "precocious identity formation" as Helfaer (1972) noted in his book *The Psychology of Religious Doubt*. His observation was of a pre-adolescent boy who used religious language constructs and faith concepts far beyond his developmental ability and therefore exhibited an identity that could not have been owned and which would likely be rejected at a later stage. Another danger of unreflected faith acquisition through sanitized story-telling is the possibility of developing the form of certainty that causes fundamentalism.

In short, the open telling of a Bible story, in which the child can wrestle with the story's meaning in the company of a parent who is comfortable with the process, is likely to develop spiritual wonder in the child.

Other research into the process of encouraging faith development in children has noted that the facilitating environment is of greater benefit than the religious environment (Worsley 2000, p.291). In other words, it is the nurturing environment encouraging a child's security that is more valuable than the particular encouragement to adopt a certain creed. This is more likely to produce a religious faith that continues into adulthood.

In the evaluation that parents sent back after completing the project it was clear across the board that the project was a good experience for *all* those who had taken part. Their reasons were mainly that they had spent more time together with their children and come across different Biblical stories not found in children's Bibles. Parents were generally impressed that their children understood so well and could articulate so much insight. One parent wrote, "we learned that children can relate to texts which we might have assumed were 'too adult' for them in terms of terminology and content."

When asked what their children had learned, respondents either mentioned the new stories that they had encountered or the fact that the Bible contained different genres of story. One parent wrote, "They learned that is was OK to ask questions about the stories and to express their own interpretations."

To the question, "What was bad about the experience?" most parents were keen to say that they had few negative feelings. One parent was a little worried as to how the research team might evaluate her responses. Another said that she had concern that "the younger child's disbelief that the Noah story could have happened literally might affect their acceptance of other stories."

One mother, however, had some deep concerns. "I was deeply disturbed with the thoughts of death and fears that my child had been suffering with. It had crossed my mind to stop and select the stories myself. After some thought, I felt it was better to have these thoughts out in the open and dispel them with discussion. I was fearful that my unbelieving partner would use our son's unhappiness to bolster up his argument that 'Church was evil' and stop all the input."

The next question asked whether the child had experienced negative feelings and in response to this several mentioned the puzzlement expressed over the story of "Jepthah's return", though it was also stated that this concern soon passed.

One parent felt that at times the exposure to language that was "too complex" was unhelpful. In this instance the child was used to being read to from a simplified children's Bible with cartoons, even though her cognitive level was able to grapple with more advanced literature.

When asked if this experience had changed their understanding of the Bible, most parents said it had not, although a few commented that noting the difference in genres had allowed them greater flexibility in their approach to the text. One parent wrote, "The experience made us realize that we don't necessarily need to use simplified or edited children's Bibles for kids to be able to engage with the text."

To the question, "Do you think that the Bible can be meaningful to children?" there was a resounding yes. This was qualified in several instances that care had to be taken in noting the child's developmental stage. Similarly, all respondents replied that they would be willing to have a further visit from the research team to discuss the results.

Implications for school teachers

The argument for the Bible to be used more in schools has been made by Kay and Wilkins (1998) who have set out to re-adjust the inheritance of Goldman (1964, 1965), who underestimated pupils' potential for understanding scriptural narrative. They argue that, "as a text for children, the Bible offers a wealth of possibilities to teachers of Religious Education." They also recommend the usage of age-appropriate translations of the Bible to help release the natural spirituality in children. Finally, they conclude by saying that because of their openness to wonder, "Children may be better at interpreting the Bible than adults are" (p.69).

This more radical suggestion is what inspires the project "Bible Stories Between Parents and their Children". Maybe teachers can be tempted beyond the boundaries of the curriculum to be partners in releasing something of the spirituality that is natural to children. Indeed, such ideas are no longer merely speculative since Ofsted has become increasingly aware of the need for a broad spirituality to be present across the curriculum. The School Curriculum and Assessment Authority (SCAA) has written:

> The term 'spiritual development' needs to be seen as applying to something fundamental in the human condition which is not necessarily experienced through the physical sense or expressed through everyday language. It has to do with relationships with other people and, for believers, with God. It has to do with the universal search for individual identity – with our responses to challenging experiences, such as death, suffering, beauty and encounters with good and evil. It is to do with the search for meaning and purpose in life and for values by which to live. (SCAA 1995)

Bible stories are the sort of literature that can be the source from which such broader conversations can be had.

Ofsted goes even further by incorporating spiritual development under the umbrella of pupils' personal development and is beginning to be clearer at how to identify such spirituality within a recognisable nurturing environment. Again, this project would suggest that such an environment as that identified on pages 146–147 is one in which a spiritual ethos is present.

The Biblos Project (Copley 1998, 2001 and 2004) has also evidenced that the Bible has significant cultural implications even for pupils who are atheist. The findings from their six-year period of research, complete with publications appropriate to the various key stages, is recorded on the web site of The Bible Society – www.biblesociety.org.uk

Finally, simply in terms of being a collection of different books told across a long period of time, the Bible is useful as a source to enable children to distinguish between different genres. As far back as 1986, Goebbel and Goebbel noted that children from the age of six are able to identify between various literary genres in the Bible and can tell the difference between story, poetry and letters.

Therefore, for spiritual, social, moral, cultural and diagnostic reasons there is evidence to suggest that Bible stories can play a wider part in school life.

Implications for church ministers

In identifying the term "Church Ministers" this project does not merely mean the key professionals who are the public representative ministers in a given denomination (i.e. ordained priests and pastors), but the host of lay people who may work with children. These may be full-time family workers or youth ministers through to those who offer an occasional slot on the rota for Sunday school, Children's Church or the Youth Club.

A key implication is that the text of the Bible used on any given occasion is allowed to be heard in context. As has been demonstrated within the case studies of this project and in wider research, a story must be allowed to be reflected upon and not merely given a set meaning. Indeed it should be noted that key stage two children (aged 7–11) are unlikely to draw a standardized meaning from a Bible story, but will reflect on it in a way that shows their own life experience. This is argued in a more academic way in *How Children aged 9–10 Understand Bible Stories* (Worsley 2004).

Therefore the role of the Church can be that of a teller of the story as told at source, but not necessarily the custodian and sole interpreter. The Church does have its own authority and will have an interpretation of the meaning of Bible stories, but it can also be wondrous as to the fuller meaning. If it is to demonstrate such openness, the Church needs to be attentive to the insights of children engaging with scripture and encountering God. Then it will also be open to new ways of understanding the ancient text.

One way of doing this is to be seen in the work of Jerome Berryman (1995) whose engaging way of opening up the Bible is called "Godly Play". Berryman consciously draws on a seminal book by Maria

Montessori called *The Child in the Church* (1965) and an influential work by S. Calvalletti entitled *The Religious Potential of the Child* (1983). From these sources Berryman has pioneered a way of reading the Bible in a way that allows for spiritual wonder and which does not allow a pre-set meaning to dominate.

One of the ways Berryman does this is by inviting the adult to become like a child. Instead of being the keeper of the truth or the fount of all wisdom, the adult is invited to look with wonder and imagination. He writes:

> Godly play is a way to keep open the opportunity for the true self to emerge in childhood and the possibility that adults may return to where they began and begin to grow again. (p.158)

Therefore he calls upon the adult to no longer rely on reason or even belief, but to play and to wonder.

If this type of simple method is employed, imagination will be free to unlock the text and the adult and the child will be able to sit alongside as hearers and interpreters of the Bible story. This is commented upon by Cox in her Grove booklet, *Using the Bible with Children* (2000) where she says:

> If we give them (children) the skills to explore the Bible for themselves, listen respectfully to their insights and encourage them to find personal applications, then we can begin to discover together.

From an analysis of the respondents from this project to hear a child responding to Bible stories, it is clear that some parents are not comfortable in sitting alongside as facilitators whilst their children develop a meaning of the text. This calls for a deeper understanding in how the Bible stories yield their meaning. M. Pike has discussed this in an article entitled *The Bible and the Reader's Response* (2003b) in which he suggests a way to avoid "interpretative anarchy". In simple terms this means understanding engagement with the Bible will involve both exegesis (a "drawing out" of meaning from the text) and an eisogesis (a "reading into" the text of one's own personal meaning). Different schools of thought will value either end of this continuum of engagement, but the main thing is to understand that both exegesis and eisogesis are present at any level of understanding a story.

Conclusion

Having completed this initial investigation into what children actually feel and say when encountering the sacred texts of the Bible, I feel distinctly "moreish". I wonder what other insights lie beyond the boundaries of adult wisdom, whether as forgotten treasures from the past or as discarded pearls along the way.

In simple terms, the formula for "A Child Sees God" is a simple one, namely to listen to the child's viewpoint without critique – and so to rediscover primal fears, hopes and thoughts. It involves both the religious adult holding their credal faith in suspension and the secular adult holding their critical judgement in check. Both the theist and the atheist must learn from the emergent spirituality of a child making sense of stories that have been born out of the earliest oral traditions and which have been reflected upon by those religions that seek revelation from the written text.

The result of this is at times ordinary and predictable, but at other times extraordinary and revolutionary to our previous thoughts. It is, I believe, a new hermeneutic, a way to finding young insights from old sources. It is perhaps the only way of understanding that ancient barb of the Christian Messiah when he chided his adult followers, "Unless you become like a child, you will not enter the Kingdom of God."

Appendix 1

Authentic Texts for Children

For the purpose of finding out how children relate to the Bible, only an original Biblical text (rather than one adapted for children) has been used in this project. Although there runs the risk of the story not being immediately understood, the actual text has been deemed to be of considerable importance in the transmission of the story. This recognizes that the stories will have originated in an oral tradition before they were ever written and the fact that they have been caught upon the printed page gives them a new and more permanent dimension.

It also recognizes that value is given by the worshipping community onto the sacred text of the Bible. The Old Testament books initially emerged from being told within community contexts as a collection of scrolls. In turn these proceeded to be edited and added to by a variety of copyists over time. It is generally believed that no uniform canon of scrolls existed within the early Church, with various synagogues storing different scrolls. For example, a synagogue in Jerusalem might have the scroll of Isaiah, but not the minor prophets in their collection or a synagogue in Damascus might have the books of the Kings but not of the Chronicles. A greater consideration of this idea is discussed in Wurtwein's *The Text of the Old Testament* (1979) who details that after the oral traditions were written (730BC onwards), the Israelites became known as "the people of the book", emphasizing past knowledge over new revelation. The written text then became standardized, though it would still be amended by scribes.

Wurtwein goes on to identify that the fixing of books into a canon was not made until The Council of Jamina in AD 100. Until that time, considerable variance in texts or editions of texts will have been known. Of course, this Council will have authorized texts which were later to be considered apocryphal by the 15th century reformers, who have left a legacy whereby the Roman Catholic Church continues to read apocryphal books that Protestant churches have ceased to use.

Historically, Bibles that were specifically printed for children have been read since the 16th century. They have variously included pictures, headings, comments and even questions to open up the text. The issues arising from children reading Bible stories have troubled theologians and philosophers including Martin Luther, Desiderius Erasmus, John Locke and Friedrick Schleiermacher. However, most authors and editions of children's Bibles were lesser known preachers, teachers or parents.

A detailed study into the hundreds of children's Bibles that have been printed since the 16th century has been undertaken by Ruth Bottigheimer. This volume, simply entitled *The Bible for Children* (1996) details her initial shock in the subject.

> I began to think about Bible stories after I visited a small German museum that housed Grimm family memorabilia. The director hospitably put some of the collection's displays into my hands. One was Jacob Grimm's childhood Bible story collection of 1785. I could hardly believe my eyes. Here, in a book for children, was Lot offering his virgin daughter to a rapacious mob, Abraham ready to slit Isaac's throat, and Joseph sexually importuned by his master's wife. (p.xii)

Early in this study Bottigheimer helpfully offers two models of children's Bibles as examples for what has happened over time. One was that written by the 12th century, French churchman Peter Comestor, entitled *Historia Scholastica* and the other was composed by the 16th-century German reformer Martin Luther, entitled the *Passional*.

Comestor's Bible comprised a number of stories loosely held from the Latin Vulgate, illuminated with ancient patristic drawings, whereas Luther's consisted of phrases taken verbatim from his own translation *(Sola Scriptura)* illustrated with some designs by Albrecht Dürer.

The *Historia Scholastica* included only narrative parts of the Bible, anticipating the form of children's Bibles for centuries to come. The stories were paraphrased in order to bring clarity. An example is the story of Joseph and Potiphar's wife:

> It happened however that his (Joseph's) mistress cast her eyes on Joseph and said to him, "Sleep with me." He answered her, "My master entrusted me with all his possessions except you. How then could I do that and moreover sin against my God." As Joseph tells us, it was a time of public festivity that the women were supposed to attend.

This example shows an interesting choice in story, liberally told and with references to other subsequent sources. Although the text was widely published and valued in its day, particularly appealing to university students, it was not printed after the 16th century and was spurned in Protestant areas because of its Catholic origins and its lack of faithfulness to the original text.

By contrast, Luther's pamphlet-length account of the life of Christ entitled the *Passional* to which he added some Old Testament stories, was a Bible for the laity, aimed at children and simple folk. Written in the native tongue, it relied only on the words of Holy writ for its text and so offered a different model of Bible. His choice of style was radical as he translated directly from the Hebrew and Greek.

> One must ask the mother at home, the children in the street, the people in the market, and listen how they speak and then translate accordingly. That way they will understand and notice that one is speaking German to them.

The accompanying image to the narrative was often the key to interpreting the written story. It was Luther's devotion to the literal word of God that forbade him from further tinkering with the text as Comestor had done. His high view of the Bible went on to remain the official Protestant position for the next 400 years, even if the *Passional* was not to be in demand after Luther's death.

Bottigheimer's work proceeds to examine children's Bibles by looking through the eyes of parents and children at stories of nakedness, sexual encounter, violence and miracle. It is particularly interesting to notice the choice of stories from a 21st-century perspective.

For example, the theme "Parents and Children" looks at Abraham and Isaac, David and Absalom and Lot and his daughters, all of which are highly problematic in their depiction of the parental link. Similarly the theme of sex is explored by way of Joseph and Potiphar's wife, David and Bathsheba, the rape of Dinah and the rape and murder of the Levite's wife, all of which show sexuality in terms of sinful behaviour.

These stories were shown by Bottigheimer to have been further brought to life by the accompanying illustrations taken from the Bible under consideration. The current reader will inevitably be amazed at the lurid detail that was offered to young minds. This scholarly study concludes by noting that children's Bibles express values and standards that are not universal and eternal but particular and ephemeral. Although the Bibles have appeared to be texts that are faithful to the ancient sources, the authors have produced texts that have said more about the contemporary secular values of the day than about the values of the original text.

Given these insights of history, this project has attempted to use only stories that are from the original text to ensure that the recorded encounter between children and the story is actually about sacred text and not about contemporary paraphrase or artwork. It has also attempted to use a wide variety of genres of the original text. How these genres were chosen is discussed in Appendix II.

Seven Basic Plots

Considerable reflection has gone into asking why similar stories appear all over the world. This was asked in the 18th century by Dr Samuel Johnson who said:

> How small a quantity of real fiction there is in the world; and that the same images with very little variation, have served all the authors who have ever written.

The growth of anthropology and ethnology in the 19th century saw the question of basic plots examined from different angles. Freidrich Muller (1823–1900) saw all stories as "solar myths", describing the setting and rising sun. Freud (1916) connected the contents of dreams to certain myths and attempted to identify key myths to explain the workings of the unconscious. He demonstrated that the "Oedipal triangle", a battle in which the child learns to cope with the looming presence of his or her parents, correlates with ancient myth and modern experience. Perhaps all motifs of myths can be seen in terms of sexuality – stories of rapacious mothers (like Hansel and Gretel), the escape from the womb (like Jonah and the big fish) or the discovery of final sexual fulfilment (like Cinderella or Rapunzel).

What has become clearer is that stories are ways for us to explain who we are. As an ancient source is reputed to have said, "The difference between men and animals is that men tell stories."

One of the most influential stories ever told is Plato's *Parable of the Cave* (Cooper 1997) in which he depicts a row of men, imprisoned in a cave but gazing on the back wall. On this wall they see the constant play of shadows which are in fact the images of objects passing across the fire behind them. Since this is all they see, they perceive the shadows to be reality.

After a while, one of them frees himself to look round and see the stronger light of the fire behind them. As he moves towards it he sees beyond that the greater light of the sun. Finally, after overcoming his initial blindness, he is able to gaze on the real world outside the cave.

Dazzled by this new world, he returns to his companions still transfixed by the shadows in the cave and tells them what he has seen, but he is not believed and is scorned for his views. However, he can now perceive the shapes on the wall to be no more than illusions.

This story has hugely impacted on western and Christian consciousness with its references to what is illusory and to what is real. Into this interface comes the role of the story. Stories help us reflect imaginatively on reality and to consider what is true.

This subject is explored more thoroughly in Christopher Booker's comprehensive book entitled *The Seven Basic Plots* (2004) which he subtitles *Why we tell Stories*. In this he finds the language of Jungian psychology of value to him as he traces the evolution of human beings through the capacity to imagine stories. Our development in storytelling stems in the division of our psyche between the ego and "the self" (unique in the animal kingdom), and stories are our need to reconnect the two. The ego is the centre of our consciousness, the part of our psyche through which we perceive the world and our own part in it. The self is a deeper centre in our personality which connects us with our selfless care instincts.

Working within such constructs, Booker sees that the basic plots in stories are about how the ego wrestles with the self. Sometimes it is the ego that gains the upper hand and sometimes the ego is able to reconnect with the self. Booker considers that stories to do with gods and men (such as those in the Bible), are primarily consumed with reconnection with "the one".

One of the most compelling sections in his book is his final chapter entitled "The Age of Loki" in which he traces the current dismantling of the self and cites Yeats' seminal poem:

> *Turning and turning in the widening gyre*
> *The falcon cannot hear the falconer;*
> *Things fall apart; the centre cannot hold;*
> *Mere anarchy is loosed upon the world.*
> *The blood dimmed tide is loosed; and everywhere*
> *The ceremony of innocence is drowned;*
> *The best lack all conviction, while the worst*
> *Are full of passionate intensity...*
> *And what rough beast, its hour came round at last,*
> *Slouches towards Bethlehem to be born?*

> *W.B. Yeats The Second Coming*
> (Used with kind permission of AP Watt Ltd
> on behalf of Gráinne Yeats)

This chapter follows the movement of storytelling from the 19th century, via the brave new world glimpsed between the world wars to the various re-emergence of the self. The Age of Loki is a narrative way of describing the evolution of consciousness that has brought us to a place where stories need to be re-birthed when the intelligent, amoral and ambivalent Loki is finally chained up after being the cause of widespread destruction. Booker offers no final solution since our stories can only imagine re-birth.

Booker's central thesis identifies seven plots which are described as:

- Overcoming the monster.

- Rags to riches.

- The quest.

- Voyage and return.

- Comedy.

- Tragedy.

- Re-birth.

When Bible stories were considered for this project, the initial interest was to ensure that they were told from a wide cross-section of the Bible involving both the Old and the New Testament and also including the various genres.

However, the task of identifying a wide selection of stories invariably led to a form of classifying them into:

- Texts of wonder.

- Texts of adventure and leadership.

- Texts of terror.

- Texts of justice and judgement.

- Texts of comfort and hope.

- Texts of comedy.

- Texts of mercy and forgiveness.

The very act of making such a classification was of course hermeneutical, as various people have commented. For example, some teenage girls did not find the story of Paul's shipwreck to be correctly classified as adventure because the story details a life-threatening occasion. They deemed adventure to be more to do with light-hearted swashbuckling fun. Again, some parents objected to considering the story of Balaam's ass to be one of comedy as they, far more seriously, wanted to dwell on the issues of judgement. For them the ability of the ass to observe God's actions and to speak out are literal truths and not a comic ploy by the Old Testament author, as is implied by the classification.

A later reflection has been to make possible connections between our seven-fold classification and Booker's seven plots. Although this does not fit entirely, it offers some identical matching and some close correlation.

BSP* classification	Booker's plots
Texts of Wonder	Rags to riches
Texts of Adventure and Leadership	Voyage and return
Texts of Terror	Tragedy
Tests of Justice and Judgement	The quest
Texts of Comfort and Hope	Re-birth
Texts of Comedy	Comedy
Texts of Mercy and Forgiveness	Overcoming the monster

* BSP is Bible Story Project (i.e. the research project on which this book is based)

The following shows the texts for the project seen as an overview.

Texts for the Project

(1) Texts of wonder

(a) The Creation (Genesis 1–2 v 3)

(b) Moses and the Burning Bush (Exodus 3–4 v 5)

(c) The Birth of Jesus (Luke 1 v 26–55 & 2 v 1–35)

(2) Texts of adventure and leadership

(a) David and the Mighty Men (2 Samuel 23 v 13–17)

(b) The Fall of Jericho (Joshua 2 v 1–24 & 6 v 1–27)

(c) Paul's Shipwreck (Acts 27)

(3) Texts of terror

    (a) Abraham and Isaac (Genesis 22 v 1–19)

    (b) Jephthah's Return (Judges 11 v 29–40)

    (c) Ananias and Saphira (Acts 5 v 1–11)

(4) Texts of justice and judgement

    (a) Banishment from Eden (Genesis 3)

    (b) Noah's Ark (Genesis 6–9 v 19)

    (c) The Sheep and the Goats (Matthew 25 v 31–46)

(5) Texts of comfort and hope

    (a) David and Goliath (1 Samuel 17 v 1–54)

    (b) The Resurrection of Jesus (John 19 v 13–20 v 25)

    (c) The New Jerusalem (Revelation 20 v 11–22 v 21)

(6) Texts of comedy

    (a) Balaam's Ass (Numbers 22 v 21–35)

    (b) The Unjust Judge (Luke 18 v 1–8)

    (c) The Seven Husbands in Heaven (Luke 20 v 27–40)

(7) Texts of mercy and forgiveness

    (a) Jonah (Jonah 1 & 3–4)

    (b) The Prodigal Son (Luke 15 v 11–32)

    (c) Zacchaeus (Luke 19 v 1–10).

Bibliography/Further Reading

Adams, K., Hyde, B. and Wooley, R. (2008) *The Spiritual Dimension of Childhood.* London: Jessica Kingsley.

Berryman, J.W. (1995) *Godly Play.* Minneapolis MN: Augsburg.

Bettelheim, B. (1976) *The Uses of Enchantment.* London: Penguin.

Booker, C. (2004) *The Seven Basic Plots.* London: Continuum.

Bottigheimer, R. (1996) *The Bible for Children.* London: Yale University Press.

Calvalletti, S. (1983) *The Religious Potential of the Child.* New York: Paulist Press.

Cooper, J.M. (ed.) (1997) Parable of the cave. In: The Republic, Book VII, in *Plato's Complete Works.* Wordsworth edn, S. Watt (ed), London: Hackett.

Copley, T. (1998) *Echo of the Angels: The First Report of the Biblos Project.* Exeter: School of Education, University of Exeter.

Copley, T., Lane, S., Savini, H. and Walshe, K. (2001) *Where Angels Fear to Tread, The Second Report of the Biblos Project.* Exeter: School of Education, University of Exeter.

Copley, T., Freathy, R., Lane, S. and Walshe, K. (2004) *On the Side of Angels, The Third Report of the Biblos Project.* Exeter: School of Education, University of Exeter.

Cox, R. (2000) *'Using the Bible with Children.'* Grove Booklet B15. Cambridge: Grove Books Pub.

Cox, R. (2001) Using the Bible with children. *Journal of Education and Christian Belief 5(1),* 41–49.

Donaldson, M. (1978) *Children's Minds.* Glasgow: Fontana/Collins.

Erricker, C., Erricker, J., Ota, C., Sullivan, D. and Fletcher, M. (1997) *The Education of the Whole Child.* London: Cassell.

Fawcett, M. (1998) *Learning Through Child Observation.* London: Jessica Kingsley Publishers.

Fowler, J. (1981) *Stages of Faith.* San Francisco: Harper and Row.

Francis, L.J. (2000) 'Who reads the Bible? A study among 13–15 year olds.' *British Journal of Religious Education, 22(3),* 165–172.

Freud, S. (1916) *The Theory of Dreams.* Collected Papers Vol III. London: Hogarth.

Frost, R. (1973) *Modern Poems,* (ed. Ellmann). New York: Norton.

Goebbel, R. and Goebbel, G. (1986) *The Bible: A Child's Playground.* London: SCM.

Goldman, R. (1965) *Readiness for Religion.* London: Routledge and Kegan Paul.

Goldman, R. (1964) *Religious Thinking from Childhood to Adolescence.* London: Routledge and Kegan Paul.

Haynes, J. (2002) *Children as Philosophers.* London: Routledge.

Helfaer, P.M. (1972) *The Psychology of Religious Doubt.* Boston: Beacon Press.

Kay, W. and Wilkins, R. (1998) Reading for Readiness. *Journal of Education and Christian Belief 2(1),* 65–69.

Kelly, G.A. (1955) *The Psychology of Personal Constructs* (2 Vols). New York: Norton.

Kierkegaard, S. (1843) *Fear and Trembling.* Denmark: Johannes de Silentio.

Meek, M., Warlow, A. and Barton, G. (eds) (1977) *The Cool Web – The Pattern of Children's Reading.* London: The Bodley Head.

Montessori, M. (1965) *The Child in the Church.* St Paul MN: Catechetical Guild.

New Revised Standard Version of the Bible (1997) *The HarperCollins Study Bible with Apocrypha,* London.

Piaget, J. (1948) *The Moral Judgement of the Child.* Glencoe: Free Press.

Piaget, J. (1952) *The Origins of Intelligence in Children.* New York: International University Press.

Piaget, J. (1954) *The Construction of Reality in the Child.* New York: Basic Books.

Pike, M. (2003a) Belief as an obstacle in reading the Bible. *Journal of Beliefs and Values 24(2),* 155–164.

Pike, M. (2003b) The Bible and the reader's response. *Journal of Education and Christian Belief, 7(1),* 37–51.

Rizutto, A.M. (1981) *The Birth of the Living God.* London: Chicago University Press.

SCAA (1995) *Spiritual and Moral Development* – A Discussion Paper by Qualifications and Curriculum Authority, London. See www.curriculum.qca.org.uk

UNICEF Report (2007) *All Things Considered.*

Vygotsky, L.S. (1962) *Thought and Language.* Cambridge, MA: MIT Press.

Worsley, H. (2000) *The inner-child as a resource for adult faith development.* (Faith in Transition) Unpublished PhD Thesis, University of Birmingham, Birmingham.

Worsley, H. (2002a) The inner-child as a resource for adult faith development. *British Journal of Religious Education 24(3),* 196–207.

Worsley, H. (2002b) The impact of the inner-child on adult believing. *Journal of Beliefs and Values 23(2),* 191–202.

Worsley, H. (2004) How children aged 9–10 understand Bible stories: A study of children at a church aided and a state primary school in the Midlands. *International Journal of Children's Spirituality 9(2)*, 203–217.

Worsley, H. (2006) Insights from Children's Perspectives in Interpreting the Wisdom of the Biblical Creation Narrative. *British Journal of Religious Education 28(3)*, 249–259.

Worsley, H. (2009) 'Through the Eyes of a Child.' In Richards, A. and Privett, P. (eds) *Angels.* London: Church House Publishing.

Wurtwein, E. (1979) *The Text of the Old Testament.* London: SCM.

Yeats, W.B. (1921) *The Second Coming.* In: *Michael Robartes and the Dancer.* Monarch Notes. London.

Index